# Return to Love

*A Guide to Inner Peace, Emotional Healing and Spiritual Transformation*

# *Yogi Kanna*

Kamath Publishing
San Ramon, CA, U.S.A.

Return to Love: A Guide to Inner Peace, Emotional
Healing and Spiritual Transformation

© 2013, 2014 Yogi Kanna

First Edition, July 2013

Second Edition, April 2014

ISBN-13: 978-0615840932

ISBN-10:0615840930

Published by Kamath Publishing

Cover design: Nithya Iyer and Aparna Kamath

Heart Chakra picture courtesy: Asun Phong

**Disclaimer:**

This book is sold with the understanding that the
author and publisher are not engaged in rendering
psychological or medical advice. If expert assistance
or counseling is required, the services of a licensed
professional should be sought. The writings in this
book are religious/spiritual in nature.

# Table of Contents

# Chapter I

## Hitting Rock Bottom - Biggest Opportunity for Change

"Pleasure puts you to sleep, pain wakes you up."
- *Dadashri*

\*\*\*

Sometimes in life, you may realize that the path you are on may or may not be the best one. However, there is little or no motivation for you to change your direction until something extraordinary happens that forces you to reassess everything that you have been doing. It can sometimes propel you to make big changes leading to a complete transformation.

Once there was a young man swimming along the shores of the Pacific Ocean when the sun was just about to set. A big wave came over him and sent him spiraling downwards several feet under water. Since it was late evening, the bottom of the ocean was just as dark as the surface and he couldn't tell which way was up and which way was down. He held his breath and kept paddling in a direction which he thought would lead him up. He panicked and started doubting if the direction was the right one. He would go one way and then the other, but couldn't make up his mind. He was running out of breath but he put his faith in his decision and kept paddling with his arms and legs hoping to rise above the surface any second. However, instead of finding the surface, he realized that he just hit rock bottom. He realized that he had headed in the wrong direction. With this revelation his path became clear: any chance of survival lay in the opposite direction he just came from. He used his legs to stand on the very bottom, bent his knees to push against the earth floor below him and thrust himself in the opposite direction. Now he knew that his direction was the right one, because it was the exact opposite of the rock bottom where he was a moment ago. He was totally convinced that he was headed upwards, and used every ounce of his strength to propel him in that direction. Soon he found himself above the surface of the ocean. He took several deep breaths and felt grateful for having made it safe.

Sometimes when you are swimming along the shores of the ocean of life, it throws a big wave that sends you spiraling downwards. It may be a life threatening disease, a failed relationship, the death of a loved one, a loss in business, a difficult financial situation or some traumatic or tragic event that catches you off-guard and leaves you in utter chaos turning your life upside down. It is not these incidents in life that make you hit rock bottom, it is the choices you make following these incidents. It is how you handle these incidents that lead you to a place where you end up. If you consider yourself a victim, wallow in self-pity and try to find solace in drugs, alcohol, food or sex to escape from the pain; or if you resort to anger, resentment, denial or hopelessness, it will suffocate your soul and gradually lead you to drown deeper and deeper. Initially you may not realize it, but one day you will hit a new low, the very rock bottom; you will then realize that a pivotal point has been reached. There will be perfect clarity in your mind that the choices you made following the big wave did not help you get back to the surface but in fact brought you to the lowest place possible: rock bottom. There will no longer be any doubt in your mind that if you are to give another chance to your soul, you will have to let go of these choices and make an alternative one. You use the bottom to thrust yourself up in the opposite direction. The very things that previously tempted you appeal to you no more, for you know where they lead to. No matter how strong the urges, you recognize that those habits, beliefs, emotions or behavior have to go for they haven't served you in the past. Once you hit rock bottom, there is no more turning back to those hurtful choices. You propel yourself upward, powered by a new sense of direction, and rise back up to the surface.

I'd like you to think of this book as a message from your own heart to help you rise back to the surface whenever you get hit by a wave, and give you the inspiration and strength to handle all future waves. The words in this book are not meant for your brain to accumulate as new information; rather they are meant to assist you in remembering that which your heart already knows to be true.

As you read each chapter, **read slowly, free of distractions, pausing and reflecting quietly.** Slow down your mind, open your heart, and let the words in the book soak your soul, serving as a gentle reminder of your highest truth. Pick up this book every once in a while and read and reflect on one or two chapters at a time. Experiment with the practices presented here, and discover the truth in your heart. Staying in touch with the truth in your heart will serve as a life-line to help you in times of need. You will find you are able to handle any waves the ocean of life sends your way and will be able to rise up to the surface over and over again. You never know when the next wave will come. Be ready!

# Chapter II

---

## The Truth Shall Set You Free

The desire for freedom is to the soul what the desire for breath is to the body. It is this deep desire for freedom that drives you to various kinds of pursuits in life.

When you deeply examine each desire, at its root you will find as its source the desire for freedom. When you desire money, you are seeking freedom; having money frees you from the worries of survival and gives you the freedom to create a lifestyle of your choice. When you desire love (human affection, not absolute love which will be discussed later in the book), you are seeking freedom; feeling loved gives you the ability to express yourself freely without the fear of rejection or condemnation. When you desire fame, again you are seeking freedom; fame seemingly makes other people love and respect you more, and gives you greater freedom to express, create and experience a world of your desire. You will find that in each desire is rooted this desire for freedom.

Without the freedom to be and express who we are, we would feel miserable and lifeless, wouldn't we? No one likes to have their freedom taken away. That's the reason we put criminals in prison as punishment. But even those of us who are not physically behind bars may feel we live in a prison of sorts. Few enjoy the freedom to live a life in harmony with their heart's true desires. Most feel restricted in some way or other. People find themselves reporting to jobs they don't enjoy, feel stuck in relationships where they don't feel loved, etc. There is something or other that people find missing in their lives.

If you have time, you don't have money; if you have money, you don't have time; if you have time and money, you don't have health; if you have time, money and health, you may not feel loved; if you have time, money, health and human-affection, you may not have wisdom!

Time, money, health, human-affection, etc., are nice to have. But without wisdom, you may find yourself clueless as to what brings true fulfillment, and may end up investing your time and energies in destructive and self-defeating pursuits.

Without wisdom you may be led to diving into activities that look attractive in the beginning but ultimately lead to stagnant waters. If you don't look before you leap, you may find yourself bound in chains, losing whatever little freedom that you once had:

- You may seek riches, thinking they will offer a pillar of support; instead they can become a burden of worry and stress.
- You may seek marriage hoping to grow wings of freedom; instead you may find yourself bound by chains of attachment and responsibilities.
- You may seek fame hoping to surf away on waves of love and adoration of many; instead you may find yourself drowned in a pool of public scrutiny, loss of privacy and personal space.

Pursuing desires led by wisdom and pursuing desires led by beliefs are two different things. When someone tells you something and you accept it as a fact without investigation, it becomes a "belief." Belief is thus second-hand knowledge, whereas "wisdom" is first-hand realization. When you lead a life based on beliefs, you lead a second-hand life. Before venturing on a journey based on beliefs propagated by society, it is wise to take the time to examine those beliefs closely and experiment with them before accepting them as "truth."

Unlike animals whose life is dominated by biological instincts driven by the desire for survival, humans have the ability to pause, question and assess before acting upon any impulse. However, when we lose touch with this human ability and revert to a herd mentality blindly allowing the instinctual drives (originating from social, biological, religious and such conditionings) to dominate our life, it turns us into a competitive species fearful of each other. Our happiness is acquired at the expense of another person's sorrow. When you lead a life driven by such instincts originating from herd mentality, you may find yourself happy at times, but sorrowful quite often. As long as you don't understand the exact causes for happiness or suffering, you will feel trapped in an uncertain world. You may begin to imagine life as a random series of events which sometimes brings joy and sometimes grief. However, life is anything but random. When you set aside all beliefs about what others have told you about life, and begin to ask yourself the deep questions, the inner wisdom in you beings to awaken.

You have to ask yourself these deep questions: Who am I? What does my heart truly desire? What is suffering? What is pleasure? What is pain? What brings true fulfillment? What is true love? etc. When you go within and discover for yourself the answers to these deep questions, you discover the truth about life. Whenever you encounter any emotion or thought, instead of acting on them instinctively or habitually, you can pause and shine the light of truth on them and investigate if they are in tune with your heart's true desire.

When you deeply realize the truth about who you really are, and what your heart truly desires, you immediately begin to see for yourself whether the path you are currently on is leading you in the direction of your highest good or away from it. Even as you read this book, take everything with a grain of salt. Do not blindly believe in anything that is written here. Experiment with the words in this book and see for yourself if they are true for you. Once you know the truth, the truth shall set you free.

# Chapter III

## Truth is a Pathless Land

"It is better to engage in one's own *Dharma* (*Swa-Dharma*), even if performed imperfectly, than to accept another's *Dharma* (*Para-Dharma*) and perform it perfectly. *Karma* performed according to one's own nature, are never affected by sinful reactions." - Bhagavad Gita, Chapter 18:47

"Truth is a pathless land." - J. Krishnamurti

\*\*\*

In ancient times, people of India practiced a religion called *Sanatana Dharma* which literally meant "Eternal Religion." It was not so much of an organized religion or belief system as much as it was a cultural value system with some principles, morals and guidelines, under whose umbrella several hundred practices existed. One of the fundamental principles of *Sanatana Dharma* was *Swa-dharma* which literally meant "Religion of the Self" or a path chosen by one's own heart.

*Santana Dharma* recognized that each person is unique and his or her spiritual journey should be guided by an inner calling of heart, and not through external imposition, as there can be no "one size fits all" formula. Because of this principle, people were encouraged to follow their own heart and relate to God or spirit in their own way.

Thus were born thousands of practices and hundreds of schools, each unique and different from the others, although there were quite a few similarities too. Under the single umbrella of *Sanatana Dharma* therefore, existed several paths to the spirit. The Four types of Vedas, six schools of *Yoga, Buddhism, Sikhism, "Hinduism," Jainism, Aghora, Tantra, etc,* were all off-shoots of what was once *Sanatana Dharma.* Each school had different sets of rituals, practices and beliefs. There was no restriction that one should follow a particular school to the exclusion of all others. There was no death penalty for apostates, nor was there any threat of hell-fire for non-believers; people were free to choose any path that their heart felt led to or their mind felt curious about. Many experimented with multiple paths and studied under different schools as led by their soul's calling. Some even became liberated sages like *Buddha, Mahavira, Guru Nanak, Sankara, Ramakrishna,* et al., and established their own schools. None of them had any intention of starting a separate religion, but their followers identified themselves with such and such schools, and some of them evolved into independent faiths.

People from the west who visited India in the early 17th century were perplexed by the variety and apparent contradictions in the various schools of religious practices of India. They observed that in these schools: some practiced physical regimens, while others sat in silent contemplation; some indulged in idol worship while others meditated on the formless spirit; some were strict vegetarians, while others not only ate meat but also sacrificed animals to deities; some were ascetic monks while others indulged with multiple partners; some practiced secluded meditation, while others performed public ceremonies. Although there were so many contrasting practices, the people seemed to be living in peace and acceptance; there was a unity among diversity. The foreigners couldn't make sense of the religion of India. So they called the people of Indus valley "*Hindus*" (the Indus valley was also called "*Al Hind*" by Arabs). And thus was born the term "Hinduism," a common label given to the "religion(s)" practiced by inhabitants of the Indus valley. Some people are still perplexed about what this "*Hinduism*" is.

Hinduism is not a religion. It was simply a label given to the culture of India under whose umbrella numerous religions and religious practices existed, many of which had little or no connection to one another. If any name is to be given to the original religion of the people of India, it ought to be *Sanatana Dharma*.

Just as parents provide education, food, and moral, physical and emotional support until a child grows up to find his or her own purpose in life; the basic purpose of *Sanatana Dharma* and other such religions was to provide loving support and guidance for their children until they grew old enough to discover their *Swa-dharma* or their own dharma, a path that resonated with their own heart.

Parents can instill into their children some values to help guide them until they are mature enough to make their own choices. This will help the children avoid making bad choices and prevent needless suffering while growing up. Similarly, *Sanatana Dharma* provided some guidelines like karma, re-incarnation, liberation from the cycles of birth and death, etc., to help guide people until they discovered their *Swa-Dharma*. These fundamental principles gave birth to several eastern religions like Buddhism, Jainism, Sikhism, etc. Every other Indian religion or school (including Yoga) that did not get a separate label was grouped under the common term of "Hinduism." Even some present day Hindus are confused over their own identity and origin as there are hundreds of practices and rituals, many seemingly contradictory to one another, all being followed in the name of one religion "Hinduism."

Just as children born of the same parents grow up into completely different individuals with completely dissimilar personalities and worldviews, *Sanatana Dharma* gave birth to many different practices which have assumed widely divergent shapes. Some evolved into practices and teachings which spread love, peace, joy, health and wisdom; while others evolved to become bizarre rituals, belief systems and superstitions.

Just as it would be incorrect for a parent to force a child into a particular profession or life choice, it would be incorrect for any religion to require followers to strictly adhere to its principles until they die, and blackmail them with hell-fire and dire consequences if they don't. Doing so is a complete disrespect to the natural longing of the soul for Self-discovery. Just as it is painful to watch certain parents unwilling to let go of control over their children even after they reach adulthood, it is painful to watch certain religions impose themselves upon their children through force, threats and violence. Some religions not only impose themselves on their own followers, but go to the extent of trying to exert influence on followers of different religions as well.

When children are growing up, they hold their parents' hands as they walk along the side of the street. It helps them feel safe. But a time comes when they let go of their mommy' and daddy's hands and become independent. Similarly, a time comes in the life of a soul, when the soul has to let go of the guiding hand of religion to explore a world of spirituality.

Religion is to follow someone else's word as truth; whereas Spirituality is to discover your own truth through inquiry, experimentation and experience. Religion has value as long as one remains a child (a young soul), but upon adulthood (becoming a spiritually mature soul) one has to make one's own discoveries. As a child, your parents may have told you "Don't talk to strangers, they may kidnap you," or "Finish your food, otherwise the Boogeyman will come and get you!" However, as you grow into an adult, if you hold onto your parents' advice that applied to you as a child, you will remain socially inept and still believe in strange superstitions! Your parents' advice may have helped you avoid trouble when you were a child, but when you grow up and mature into an adult it is time to let go of those beliefs and become your own person. Religious teachings and dogma have some value when a soul is young and immature, but as a soul matures, it is time to let go of superstitions and blind beliefs, time to adopt an attitude of scientific inquiry and experimentation; it is time to let go of bookish knowledge and theory, time to adopt practice and personal experience; it is time to let go of religion and time to adopt Spirituality.

A seeker of truth is a daughter of the great mother of all religions *Sanatana Dharma*. She is a scientist with an open mind. She neither accepts nor rejects any path without sincerely experimenting with its practices and observing the results first hand. She respects all religions as a part of her own family. Just as she desires freedom to practice her *Swa-dharma*, so does she wish for the same freedom for her brothers and sisters. Her journey may take her to different explorations, adventures and discoveries; she may experiment with different practices, beliefs, teachers, paths and organizations. She learns from them and follows what resonates with her own heart. She adopts into her life the teachings that appeal to her heart, and respectfully discards the ones that don't. Sometimes upon practicing a particular path and observing the results she may develop a deep conviction for that path; she may even choose to devote herself to that path exclusively if it resonates with her so deeply that she feels it to be inseparable from her *Swa-dharma*. But never does she judge the path of another or try to impose her views on others for she recognizes the value of her own freedom. Her mother has taught her well; she is prepared to bid goodbye to her parents and commence on her journey by herself. She is ready to move on from the world of Religion *(Para-Dharma)* into a world of Spiritual Self-discovery *(Swa-Dharma)*.

Religion and Spirituality will always have their unique places to suit the needs of different souls at different times in their evolution. Both serve their purposes and complement each other. However, no religion can stake its exclusive claim on truth, for truth is a pathless land.

# Chapter IV

---

## Experiential Wisdom: Guide to the Ultimate Path

"The path of liberation is not 'ornamental' as all others are; all other paths are like dream palaces in the sky. All other paths are ornamental paths; they have big attractions and so people flock toward them as soon as they see the attraction. There are no ornaments on the path of *moksha* (liberation) and that is why it is not discernible." - Dadashri

*** 

Joe found himself at a fork on the road, and he had to decide which direction to continue on in. One way pointed to "Worldly Success," and the other pointed to "Self-Realization." He took a few steps in the direction of "Worldly Success," but was unsure if it was the right path to take. Then he returned to the fork, and took a few steps in the direction of "Self-Realization." However, he was confused again and hesitated to go any further. He retraced his steps back to the fork. He kept going back and forth in the two directions and even after several hours, he was still at the same spot.

"I have been walking since morning, but I haven't made any progress. I can't make up my mind as to which of the two is the superior path," Joe lamented to himself.

"May I help you young man?" Joe noticed a man seated in a Lotus posture at the entrance of the road that pointed to Self-Realization. He was dressed in a simple ocher robe and his face was radiating peace.

"Who are you, kind sir?" asked Joe.

"I am a *Bodhisattva*. I have traveled far on both roads and know what lies at the end of each. The road to spiritual salvation is the true home of humanity. It is what your heart truly desires. It offers the freedom and fulfillment that every soul seeks. I came back to pass on this information to all new travelers."

Joe was encouraged. His eyes lit up at the helpful hint, "Ah! Maybe this is the direction I need to take."

"Don't listen to that old fool." A voice from across the other road shouted.

Joe turned around and saw a well-dressed man accompanied by a beautiful woman dressed in the most expensive jewelry and the finest of garments.

"The guy in the robe is a loser. He was probably lazy and didn't make it big like us on the road to Worldly Success. Look at us, look at how happy we are," he continued "We have wealth, success, fame and we love each other to death. Life is perfect. Some people are just lazy and not willing to work hard on this road. Just like the lazy fox that declared the grapes to be sour, some people give up too easily and go take the other road. What kind of fun is it to be sitting by yourself and meditating?" His wife clung to his arm lovingly as he spoke the words.

Joe was intrigued, "Wow, this road to material success sure looks appealing." But he was also a little skeptical "Do you think I can make it big too?"

"Sure you can," responded the wealthy guy. "You are young and energetic. Actually, I am looking for a new apprentice. I will teach you a thing or two if you can help me with my work."

Joe was excited. "Wow, thank you so much sir!" he looked around to see how the *Bodhisattva* monk would react to this.

"Son, everything on the path of Worldly Success is temporary," the *Bodhisattva* said to him. "Moments of pleasure are followed by long intervals of pain. What is yours today becomes someone else's tomorrow."

He continued: "When your back is toward the sun and you face in the direction of the shadows, the more you chase the shadows, the more the shadows run away from you. Similarly there is no lasting peace on the path of chasing Worldly Success. But when you stop, turn around and face the sun and walk toward the light, the shadows will chase you. Similarly, when you turn toward your Self on the path of Self-Realization, contentment and peace will follow you. Upon Self-

Realization, you can play with the things of the world if you so wish. However, most are so content upon Self-Realization that worldly success hardly matters anymore after that. You will find many with Worldly Success on the path to Self-Realization; yet, seldom will you find anyone with Self Realization on the path that chases Worldly Success ..."

The wealthy man interrupted him: "Don't listen to that loser. As I said, he was probably lazy, and didn't make it big, and is dissing this path. He himself is a failure, and he doesn't want others to succeed either. You will make it big like me. Come with me, I will show you how."

Joe paused for a moment, again studying the face of the *Bodhisattva* to see if he was indeed a loser like the wealthy man suggested. The *Bodhisattva* smiled back. "Son, go with the wealthy man, and pursue the path of Worldly Success. Right now the path of Self-realization is not for you," he said. "If you travel this path halfheartedly, your mind will be disturbed by thoughts of the other path and it will trouble you whenever you face difficult challenges on this one. Go travel the other path and see for yourself where it takes you. You will know for yourself whether it leads you to a place of true contentment or to a place of strife and struggle. Upon observing the consequences you can either carry on further at a faster pace or you can turn back and choose this other path with full conviction. Let your heart be your guide; it will lead you to your true home. "

*** 

The natural instinct of the sub-conscious mind is to run after things that look and sound attractive. However, looks can be deceptive. What looks attractive today may seem like a very bad choice tomorrow. Often when you are immature, the impulse is to go after the most popular or the most attractive choice. Instant gratification and pleasure take precedence over long-term consequences. But after you have been subjected to a lot of beatings in life, the suffering you undergo (or witness) kindles wisdom and insight that helps you discriminate between true and false paths. But until that discriminatory wisdom awakens in you, you have to experiment, experience, observe and learn from the consequences. As you keep doing that, you will reach a deeper understanding of what your Soul truly desires.

The way you go about doing this can be summarized in four steps:

## Step 1: Acknowledge your current desires.

Any unfulfilled desire carries within itself an element of sorrow. So if there is any desire within you that is suppressed, denied or unfulfilled it will bring out the sorrow that it contains. The first step is to acknowledge all your current desires. There are no "right" or "wrong" desires, for all of them, as we have seen are rooted in the desire for freedom. You simply have to inquire and recognize whether these desires are driven by instincts that seek instant gratification, or are in accord with your heart's true longing. Sorting out the good seeds from the bad ones is an important first step that determines the quality of a harvest. Similarly sorting out your heart's true desire from fleeting desires (that don't lead to anything meaningful) is important in shaping the quality of your life.

## Step 2: Resolve conflicting desires.

If one desires to eat junk food everyday but also desires good health, this presents two conflicting desires. Junk food every day and good health cannot go together, just as staying up late and waking up early don't mix well. Hate and Love cannot go together either. It is important to resolve conflicting desires; otherwise there will be confusion and suffering. Just as peace can never be the result of war, fulfillment cannot be the result of harboring conflicting desires. If one desire is suppressed at the expense of pursuing another desire which is in opposition to the former, the sorrow from the suppressed desire will prevent one from enjoying the gratification of the other. Hence it is important to identify and resolve conflicting desires.

**Step 3: Once you have recognized your true desires (present ones), gratify them and experience them.**

If you have properly resolved all other conflicting desires, this step should be fairly straightforward. All it requires is focus, discipline and patience. Opportunities, people and situations will present themselves at appropriate times if your desires are truly focused and not opposed to each other. Usually desires are easier to fulfill when they are focused on inner fulfillment rather than on external achievement, for inner fulfillment is usually focused on the Self, whereas external achievement is focused on beating the competition. Desires which are too externally focused and in competition with the desires of other people (resulting in one winner and many losers), usually take longer to accomplish, a Pyrrhic victory at best. However, it is possible to gratify even such desires with enough investment of focused time, effort, and resources combined with patience and perseverance.

## Step 4: Live the consequences of gratifying your desires.

Upon gratifying your desires and seeing where they have taken you, you will gain deeper insight into your desires. You can ask yourself these questions: Did gratification of these desires lead you to a place of lasting contentment and peace, or did it increase greed and discontent? Did it take you to a place of true fulfillment and harmony, or did it lead to a place of stress and disharmony? Did it result in temporary pleasure, or did it yield lasting joy? Was the investment in time, energy and resources worth it?

Based on the consequences, you will either choose to let go of your present course if it hasn't led you to the place where you really wanted to go, or you will seek to move further down the same path if you got positive affirmation through your experiences. Either way, there will be more clarity and energy on the path forward.

Thus you will move deeper into the discovery of what your heart truly desires. You will discover who you truly are. As you experience and reflect on the consequences of your actions, life will become simpler and your goal will become clearer and easier to pursue.

Through this process of experimentation, experience and observation of consequences you will gain a deeper insight into what freedom truly means. However, to make life simpler, try limiting your experiments to the realm of *sattvic* or harmonious actions. Avoid getting involved in actions that can cause harm either to others or to yourself; try to stay away from drugs, intoxicants and illicit sex. Of course you are free to experiment with them as well, but it will save you a lot of heartache and pain if you just learn from other people's mistakes rather than to make ones of your own.

Human life is short. It can sometimes be more efficient to learn from other people's mistakes in addition to your personal experience so that you don't have to spend your entire lifetime repeating the mistakes already committed by your ancestors and peers. Yes, it is very important to get insight and wisdom from firsthand experience, but, this experience can also be gained through the process of compassion. Compassion is the ability to empathize with others. Sympathy is to feel sorry for someone; however, empathy is to feel what the other person (or living being) is going through. The more we are able to empathize and feel what the other is feeling, the more we are able to relate to others and harbor desires that are most harmonious with the collective whole. The less empathy a person has, the more violent and selfish are his desires and action towards others. A psychopath is an extreme example of someone who has lost his ability to empathize with the pain of another, and actually may draw pleasure from hurting others.

Empathy allows us to connect with the true essence of our spirit. By cultivating empathy and compassion, we can tap into the wisdom gained from the collective mistakes of our human ancestors and peers. It is this trait that led sages like Gautama to become a Buddha. Gautama was brought up in a royal family and pampered with wealth, luxuries and pleasure; he was well shielded from the suffering of the common masses. However, one day when he took a trip outside his palace and saw the common people experiencing sickness, old age and death, his compassionate heart was able to connect with their suffering and get a deep insight into the human condition. He was able to see that the way he was living life was a futile one which would ultimately lead to the same sickness, old age and death. He decided to give up his prince-hood and went out in search of Self-Realization. Although he had never experienced much suffering as a prince, having compassion allowed him to connect with the suffering of others and learn from it.

When you keep listening to your heart as you go through different experiences in life, and as you witness the experiences of others with the eyes of compassion, it will awaken inside you an experiential wisdom which brings great clarity, understanding and peace. Let that inner wisdom guide you to the ultimate path that takes you closer to what your heart truly seeks.

# Chapter V

## The Purpose of Spiritual Practice

I met Scott at a *Pranayama* class that I was teaching. At the beginning of the class, as we sat in a circle, I requested that everyone introduce themselves and briefly state their intentions for attending the class. When his turn came, Scott mentioned that he had a moving near-death experience (NDE) that led him to seek spiritual practices that could help him to reconnect with the wonderful state he experienced during the NDE. I was intrigued, and after the class, asked him if he could share with us his entire NDE experience. He generously obliged. Here's what I recollect from his story:

\*\*\*

Scott's health had been progressively getting worse. His blood pressure was steadily increasing and his heart condition was rapidly deteriorating. On one fateful day he had a massive heart attack. It started as a steady pain in his left arm that slowly radiated to his shoulder before he realized that it was actually emanating from his heart. He found himself gasping for breath and soon found his heart in immense pain. His friends rushed him to the emergency ward of the nearest hospital. The pain was becoming unbearable and at the moment of greatest anguish when Scott was starting to fear the worst, he suddenly felt lighter, pain-free and found himself floating in mid-air. He looked down and noticed that his mortal body was still lying down in the bed, motion-less, dead. He could see that people were doing CPR to his body and trying to revive him. He felt himself rising up higher and higher and eventually flew out through the ceiling into the open sky. He proceeded to fly even higher and felt as if he was passing through a tunnel at an incredible speed and was being catapulted into a different realm.

He came to a sudden stop and found himself expanding into infinite space, merging with a being of infinite bliss. Although in great awe of this mighty being of bliss, he recognized himself to be non-separate from it and allowed his heart to completely melt in this joy of reunion. He noticed that all boundaries disappeared, and everywhere he looked, there was endless love and endless joy. It was so incredibly blissful that everything felt perfect "as is." He also found that he had access to infinite universal knowledge. Any question that would come to him would be answered almost instantly. It was perfect beyond imagination and he just let himself float in the vast ocean of bliss with no cares whatsoever. He didn't know how long he had been there in that state of oneness with the all-knowing and all-loving infinite being, when a voice suddenly spoke to him: "You are not ready. Go back." He was in such a blissful state that no request was unacceptable to him. He found himself saying "OK. No problem!" and the next moment he found himself jolted back into his mortal body. He woke up to see a team of nurses and doctors administering shocks to his body by pressing metal pads against his chest. "It worked," someone screamed. "His heartbeat is returning to normal. He is regaining consciousness." And so he was. However, only a part of him was conscious of this world around him; the rest of his being was still blissfully unaware of his surroundings. The bliss that he experienced from the brief communion with the infinite being, was still lingering in his conscious awareness.

His body regained health and he relayed the experience to a few close friends. They urged him to seek help for they saw that it might be quite traumatic to return to the normal world from the ethereal world. He ignored their suggestions, convinced that he was perfectly all right. He went about his activities still floating around in bliss.

A week or so later, when he woke up one morning, he perceived a completely different world. Gone was all the bliss from the NDE; he was back in full ego-consciousness, completely identified with the body and the problems of the world. "Where am I?" he screamed to himself. "What is this shit hole?"

He found himself stuck in a scary place filled with fear, frustrations and worries. The pain of separation from the all-knowing and all-loving state he had been given a glimpse of just a week or so ago, was unbearable. He took out a gun, pointed it to the side of his forehead and was about to pull the trigger. He reasoned that killing the body would enable him to return to the infinite source. "Wait," a voice from within warned him. "What if I pull the trigger and somehow the bullet spirals around missing the important parts of my brain; and when I arrive at the universal consciousness, if the voice tells me again 'Go back. You aren't ready,' not only will I have to come back to this rotten place, but also will I be stuck in a disabled body with brain damage!" It was not an appealing thought. So he put the gun down and decided it was not a risk worth taking. He started pursuing other means to get in touch with the infinite source, spiritual practices like meditation and yoga. Through these, he hoped to re-establish contact with the essence of his true being. He may not have been ready to completely reunite with the infinite source; however, he realized that it didn't mean that he must be banished in permanent exile until he was fully ready. He could re-connect with the essence of his true being through spiritual practice.

\*\*\*

The human drama can sometimes be quite a nightmare. If we lose touch with the essence of who we truly are and where we come from, it can lead us into deep identification with the human drama leading to a state of depression and despondency. As illustrated in Scott's story above, spiritual practice is a way for us to re-establish contact with our true Self, deathless spirit. Our true nature is that of abundant peace-bliss-love. In our true Self also resides abundant wisdom, and tapping into this state every now and then gives us the necessary wisdom and strength to surf through the drama of human life.

Recall a bad dream that you may have had in the past. Recall how relieved you felt when you woke up from that dream and realized that whatever happened was just a dream and not real. As the dream was in progress though, it seemed quite real, did it not? Why then do we call that a dream and not reality? Because whatever happened, even if it seemed real for an hour or two, has no significance or bearing on your waking life; it only had significance for the duration of the dream. Similarly, isn't your present-day waking life a dream of sorts? Yes, it seems to be real for the 70-100 years that it lasts. However, what are 70-100 years in the context of the eternal life of your Soul? It is only a dream. We come to realize that this life as an embodied human being is only a dream when seen in the context of infinite existence as pure spirit.

But when we lose touch with the immortal eternal essence of our spirit, this short dream starts to seem a lot more important. We start taking this dream life too seriously and life becomes a struggle. We start developing attachments, cravings, fears, jealousies, frustrations and find ourselves struggling and competing for dream objects and dream achievements.

Through spiritual practice, when we remind ourselves of our true nature, life becomes a joyful play where we can assume different human roles without taking any of it too seriously.

When we retain touch with the reservoir of love within, we are less dependent on the people and things of this world to fulfill us. It is much easier to forgive our transgressors and let go of seemingly difficult conditions. We realize that the purpose of life is not to seek joy or love; we realize that life is simply a vehicle of expression for the wonderful being of joy and love that we already are. Let's reclaim the wonderful glory of "who we really are." Let's reconnect with our true spiritual nature that knows no sorrow or suffering and is ever established in infinite bliss and love. Let's commence our spiritual practice, now.

# Chapter VI

## Return to Love, Your True Home

Given the choice between the warmth of love and the heat of suffering, which one would you pick?

The warmth of love would be the obvious choice, wouldn't it?

Your heart instantly recognizes the feeling of love, for love is your true home. When you are immersed in love, radiating and receiving love, you are surrounded by friendly companions like ease, lightness and joy.

When you step away from this true home of yours and embody non-loving thoughts toward anyone or in response to any situation, you will find yourself in foreign territory surrounded by strangers like unease, heaviness, stress and suffering. Your heart immediately starts longing to return home, to return to love.

Although love indeed is our true home, we often lose our way when we spend too much time away from our true Self, as illustrated in the story below:

\*\*\*

There was a young prince who was heir to a kingdom that stretched over a thousand miles. He used to visit the streets of the kingdom and play with the kids there. He started spending so much time on the streets that he forgot that he was a prince. He would sleep over at his friends' place, and eventually lost his way back to the palace and started living on the streets. After daily play, some kids on the street would go begging, while others would steal from wealthier people. The prince joined these kids in such activities, and started begging and stealing himself. One day, three kids and the prince got caught while trying to steal from a wealthy traveler. They were brought to the royal court for justice.

The king was shocked to see his own son in such a state. "Oh my child, what happened to you?" He asked, "Have you forgotten that you are a prince? Why would you engage in such petty activities while you are the heir to such a vast kingdom? Why would you want to steal trivial possessions from other people while your own home is a storehouse of priceless treasure?"

*** 

Like the prince in the story above, all of us are born into the royalty of love. If you look at infants and young toddlers, you will notice how filled with love they are. Rooted in their true nature of unconditional love, infants and young children flow with life like a gentle stream; they easily let go and release the past moment and open themselves fully and lovingly to "this moment." They are so in touch with their natural state of priceless love that it doesn't take much to make them happy; just give them a cheap spoon and they will take great delight in banging the spoon repeatedly on the table! They take joy even in the simplest of things: running around in nature, playing in the mud, exploring the things in the kitchen, etc. Their joy comes not from the things of the world, but from their connectedness with love, our true home that we all were born in. The things of the world are to them mere playthings; they don't have any serious attachment to any of them.

Just as the prince in the story above lost his way after spending too much time away from the palace, we often lose touch and forget our true essence of love, our birth home, when we spend too much time away from it growing up in association with adults who are lost in the maze of thinking. The kids who taught the prince to beg are none other than thoughts of insufficiency and self-pity in association with whom we start begging for attention and appreciation from others. The three kids who got the prince to steal were thoughts of lust, envy and greed. As a result of the forgetfulness of this lofty state of love and association with thoughts in the head, smaller things in life start looking a lot more important than they really are. We start worrying, arguing and striving for trivial things and risk losing touch with our true Self, the precious kingdom within.

Life is "what is." As children, we loved "what is," we loved life unconditionally and flowed with it regardless of what shape or form it took. But as we grew up, we forgot love and inherited thought. Thought is just an idea of what life "should be," "could be" or "should have been." Behind every thought, there is constant effort to judge or change "what is." Thoughts attempt to oppose the present, change the past or control the future. This constant "doing-ness" drains our energy and tires us whenever we allow ourselves to get carried away by thinking. When you are trapped in thought, you are caught up in your head space disconnected from your heart, disconnected from Life.

"We often find ourselves in situations where we cannot stop thinking about the pain of the past or concern about the future; we seldom experience peace except for few brief moments in a day when thoughts stop on their own accord after they have been obeyed. In addition, thoughts have the ability to magnify a painful experience a hundred-fold by playing it over and over again in our head. Even if we are in beautiful surroundings, we find it hard to bring ourselves to enjoy the moment when we are drowned in the thoughts of misery." - Yogi Kanna, Nirvana: Absolute Freedom

Humanity suffers from this disease of compulsive thinking. This disease has become so prevalent that it has become the norm. But just because it is "normal" to keep thinking doesn't make it "natural." Our natural state into which we were born is that of love, and as we noted in the beginning of the chapter, love is always accompanied by lightness, peace and joy. Every human heart naturally desires to return to Love, our true home, and return to this lightness, peace and joy, our true companions. Yet, this is seldom experienced when we are drowned in thoughts in the head, disconnected from the heart that loves. Lost in thought, we find ourselves surrounded by strangers like heaviness, stress and suffering.

Thought can be a useful tool for relative worldly activities, just as a hammer is useful to a carpenter. The carpenter puts the hammer aside when he is done with his work, but most people continue to keep thinking throughout the day even when the presence of thought is not required. Imagine if a carpenter were to carry his hammer around everywhere and greeted every person by tapping their head with the hammer, would that be a sane thing to do? Yet, this is exactly what we do with our thoughts. We cannot bring ourselves to stop thinking even when it serves no useful purpose. The tool which is useful in certain situations becomes a curse when it dominates our life. It is the desire to get away from this unnatural state of compulsive thinking that leads humans to seek escape and entertainment in music, movies, alcohol, sex, food, etc. However, any attempt to escape only gives temporary relief. Even deep sleep, the only time that humans are able to completely let go of thinking and rest in true being, becomes difficult to come by when one is lost in a maze of thinking during the day. When we give thoughts a lot of attention during the day, they gain so much energy that they become dreams and nightmares and continue to assault us even in our sleep. Sometimes, thinking becomes so dysfunctional that these nightmarish thoughts can deprive people of even a moment of rest, create terrible emotions in their body and even drive a person to suicide in a desperate attempt to escape. It is the desire to return to our natural state of Love that drives some people to take this most drastic step to escape the painful emotions created by dysfunctional thinking.

"Suicide does not solve the problem either; it exacerbates the problem. The suffering is passed on to the kin of the person who commits suicide, leaving them with even more misery to handle than what was already on their plates." – Yogi Kanna, *Nirvana: Absolute Freedom*

Before these thoughts lead us to far away from our natural state, let's disassociate from these crazy thoughts now. Let's let go of the thoughts in our headspace and return to our true home, to the love in our heart space.

Daily meditation (spiritual practice) is the key to keep reminding ourselves of where we truly come from. We should aspire to set aside at least 10% of our waking time to retreat into the cave of our hearts in solitude and experience the bliss of the Self. That amounts to a minimum of about 1.5 hours of time spent in spiritual practice every day.

Just as the prince in the earlier story lost his way home after spending too much time away from the palace, we risk losing touch with our true nature when we don't spend at least 10% of our time in meditation. Whenever I have slackened my spiritual practice and lost myself in the activities if the world, I've invariably lost touch with the abundant reservoir of love within. As a result of dwelling too long in the head space, thinking and judging, I would fall from the grace of the heart space and engage in behavior totally alien to my true nature. It took me several journeys to hell and back to realize that our true nature of unconditional love was way too precious to lose touch with.

Some may ask "Is meditation in solitude necessary? Can't we simply stay aware of thoughts during the day, and release them as they arise in interactions with others?" Well, do you think musicians can play wonderfully in an orchestra without practicing in private? Can a champion athlete perform well just by showing up in a tournament? Musicians and athletes devote several hours every day in solitary practice, the results of which we get to see in an orchestra or a game. Practicing letting go of thoughts in solitary meditation where we don't have any external distractions prepares us for more challenging real-life situations when we are provoked or are under pressure. Daily practice is the key to mastery. When a master seems to abide in perfect joy and radiate unconditional love even in the midst of challenging circumstances and trying people, it is the result of devotion to the practice of solitary meditation and of connecting to the ocean of love within.

When we bask in the love of our true Self every day through meditation, it reminds us of the innate wealth that remains buried within. It reminds us how the things of this world are not something worth striving for; they are simply playthings for our spirit to have fun with. With this new understanding, it is much easier for us to remain in tune with unconditional love, our natural state. It feels very natural and organic to let go of unloving thoughts and resistance that lead us to a place of suffering. It becomes much easier to anchor ourselves to the highest truth when faced with challenging events and tumultuous periods in life. When you are in touch with the love within through daily meditation, it is easy to contrast it with the suffering of entering the non-loving space, and easy to choose the higher of the two.

Spend enough time every day basking in the ocean of love. Stay anchored in that feeling of love in your heart throughout the day. When you do this, you will flow through life like a river no matter how hard the obstacles. Where there is love, there is a way. Return to love now; your heart is waiting.

Question: You say that meditation gives us a glimpse into our true nature of unconditional love and breaks the spell of compulsive thinking that make us judgmental and non-loving. However, there seems to be some people who meditate regularly, yet they seem to be more judgmental, bitter and egotistical than most other people who don't meditate. How do you explain this?

Answer: When people try to reduce weight and go on a crash diet, they may slim down quite a bit during the diet, but once the diet is over they may binge on twice the amount of food and end up heavier than ever. Similarly, it is possible for the ego to become inflated as a result of certain meditation practices, especially if done with an incorrect attitude and faulty understanding.

The true purpose of meditation is to reconnect with and abide in our true nature of unconditional love. It is to choose the loving heart over the judgmental head.

Love is not a diet, it is a lifestyle.

When meditation is used for some temporary stress relief during the day, it is no better than an escape or entertainment and will cause no lasting change. One might as well go watch T.V. or listen to some songs on the radio. For the length of time one is on the meditation cushion, one may experience some peace; but as soon as one gets off the cushion, the mind reverts to thinking and judging. The power over one's mental state achieved during meditation may be seized upon by the ego as proof of one's superiority over others, which will cause the judgmental thoughts to be even more pronounced than usual. Eventually such a practitioner will lose all peace and revert to a state of suffering.

For lasting change, one has to adopt love into one's life-style by choosing the loving heart over the judgmental head throughout the day, and not just on the meditation cushion. Right attitude and self-honesty are very important for those who desire to reunite with their true nature of Love and to experience lasting joy and fulfillment. This is discussed in greater length in the chapters "Fake Enlightenment vs. True Liberation Parts One & Two."

# Chapter VII

## The Flame of Love: Part One

It was the summer of 2003 and I was traveling by bus in India to visit a small town in Tamilnadu. I was carrying with me a book titled *"The Awakening of Intelligence."* The author, or rather the speaker (as the book was a transcript of his talks) J. Krishnamurti, talked about observing without an observer. He suggested an exercise of looking at trees, birds and people without using the filter of thought. He said if we kept looking without labeling or interpreting, something special would happen. I was intrigued by this. I was seated by the window, and it was a good opportunity to try this experiment suggested by Krishnamurti.

As I looked out the window at the scenery passing by, I noticed thoughts appearing in my mind, interpreting what I saw. "The countryside in India is beautiful, but why do my fellow Indians throw garbage everywhere without consideration for hygiene and the natural environment?" One thought led to another: "There's so much poverty, corruption and overpopulation here. And so many people seem to have little regard for punctuality and law and order. There's much India can learn from the West in this regard. What's becoming of this great culture? What can be done to solve these issues?"

I realized I was getting carried away by thoughts, and brought myself back to the simple exercise of looking out the window without interpretation or comparison. I had been thinking about the problems faced by the world for many years toward no useful end. I hadn't solved any of my own personal problems by such thinking or worrying, let alone problems of global scale. I was open to trying something new. I was really intrigued by the promise in the book that something special would happen if I simply kept looking without the filter of thoughts. So I decided to give it a sincere try.

Whenever I noticed a thought appear in my mind trying to compare or interpret or label what I was looking at, such as "Why is this...." or "Isn't that a paddy field..." I would simply let go of any effort to complete it, and turn my attention back to the scenes that appeared through the window. I wasn't making any special effort to look, for I realized that the desire to concentrate on something is just another thought. As I kept letting go of thoughts, and I let my attention naturally and effortlessly rest upon the view outside, the thoughts slowed down. As I continued looking for another hour or two, I suddenly felt a heavy weight lift off my head, and a feeling of lightness and joy descend into my heart! It was a pleasant, intimate feeling, yet something that felt as if it had been long forgotten. It was the first time since childhood that I felt joy in my heart independent of the situation at hand. In fact, under normal circumstances, if I had carried on interpreting the same situation with thoughts, I would have felt anything but joyful. How was it that simply looking without the interpretation of thought rekindled a long-lost feeling in my heart?

The answer to this mystery is revealed once we investigate how thought operates.

What is thought? Pause for a minute and try to answer this for yourself before you read on.

Thought is a response from memory, isn't it? Anything you see, hear or experience gets captured in the brain as a memory (an image, sound or feeling).

When you look at or hear something new, something unlike anything you have ever seen or heard or felt before, it captivates your attention. You are able to be fully present to "what is" with no disturbance from thought. Your mind stops for an instant in amazement to investigate: "What is this new thing!?" There is a moment of silence when your heart opens itself fully to experience "what is." This moment is a moment of love, a joyful communion with "what is" experienced by your heart. But when you repeat the experience several times, the memory of the former experience starts playing in your head even as the actual image (or sound) reaches your eye (or ear). The thought of the previous experience prevents you from enjoying a direct relationship with the present moment. The thought, the memory compares itself with "what is" and offers a commentary on what's going on.

As a new born child, everything looked new to you, and every moment was a moment of love in which your heart was fully present to "what is," your eyes, ears and hands looking and exploring everything with loving curiosity. But as you grew older and kept looking at the same things, the memory of those experiences started playing in your mind as thoughts. Gradually you started looking at everything through the filter of these thoughts and completely forgot the experience of love. It was only during certain moments when you experienced something radically new, a new relationship, a new house, a new car, a new achievement or a new drug, that your mind became totally silent, allowing the heart to open. But with time, even those moments became fewer and further between as every experience became corrupted with thought. Looking at the same person or listening to the same song wasn't the same joyful experience that it once used to be.

When you thus associate with the thoughts in your head, you lose the ability to love. What once used to be a steady flame of love becomes a tiny flicker. An average human being completely forgets the experience of true love by the time he or she is a fully grown adult.

I was no different. Prior to this bus ride I had almost completely forgotten the feeling of true love. This bus ride in 2003 was a re-initiation into love. As I kept looking out the window without interpreting or labeling what I saw with thought, it rekindled the flame of love in my heart. I realized that love was indeed my natural state, and compulsive thinking was an unnaturally acquired habit. The experience lasted only a few seconds. The moment I tried to hold on to the feeling, it disappeared. The desire to hold on was another thought in the head that disconnected me from the heart. Although the experience was brief, it made a lasting impression on me. It inspired me further on this journey to free myself from compulsive thinking and reclaim my natural state of peace, bliss and love. As I became more proficient at letting go of thoughts in the head, and keeping my heart open to "what is," the moments of pure love and joy thus experienced became longer and more frequent. Upon returning to love, I was able to perceive the inner beauty of the things and people I looked at. Beauty lies in the eyes of the beholder. When I looked through the filter of thoughts, judging and comparing what I saw, things seemed to need a lot of improvement. When I looked through the eyes of love free of thoughts, everything looked perfect; everyone looked beautiful. It was thought that made things look "good" or "bad" by comparing "what is" with "what should be." Free of thoughts, abiding in the heart space as love, "what is" is transcendental beauty.

Return to love now. The view is beautiful from here.

The next time you travel as a passenger in a train, bus or car, look out through the window without interpreting or labeling what you see with thoughts. Look in a relaxed manner. Empty all knowledge and look with the innocence of a one-year-old child. Knowledge is memory, and memory recalled is thought. The moment you say "I know something," you become one with a thought. When you look at something with the attitude "I know this," you are really looking at the thought, not at the actual thing that you claim to know. When you realize this truth that whatever you knew was the past, a memory, and the only thing you can honestly say about the present moment is "I don't know anything," your mind empties itself, your heart opens and you're able to look through the eyes of a one-year-old. A one-year-old doesn't pretend to know something he looks at; he doesn't expect anything from it, for he doesn't know what to expect; he doesn't fear what he sees, for he knows not what to fear. He looks with an empty mind, in pure curiosity and utter amazement. As you return to that childlike innocence and look with an open heart, in that moment you will reawaken to the feeling of true love. Your heart will light up in joy in recognition of this flame of love. But don't try to hold on to the feeling, for it's not something the mind can conceive or comprehend or capture with memory. It is real and living, unlike a lifeless thought. Mental activity or effort to label or hold on to it will only serve to disconnect you from that feeling of true love. This flame of love is rekindled by the grace of your true Self, which is patiently waiting for you to awaken from the dream of thoughts into the reality of love. When you remain sincere in your desire to reawaken to your true nature of love, and become humble and innocent like a baby, this grace will enter your heart and help you rekindle that long lost feeling you truly yearn for. Once this flame of love is re-lit in your heart, even if only for a brief moment; things will never be the same again.

# Chapter VIII

## The Flame of Love: Part Two

Imagine if you were raised in poverty and lived in deplorable conditions. You may not be as bothered by physical suffering around you because you have become accustomed and desensitized to suffering from experiencing it day after day. However, imagine if you suddenly became really wealthy and got to experience the best of luxuries, comfort and social status for a few years. If you were put back on the dirty streets and left to struggle for bare necessities, the pain of returning to poverty would be enormous, wouldn't it?

Similarly, before one is touched by the flame of love, one is hardly bothered by the stress and suffering that accompanies living in a non-loving place. Radiating and receiving non-loving thoughts, feelings and actions is considered a normal part of life's "struggle" in the modern-day society. People are okay with suffering as long as it is within limits and can be numbed by drugs, alcohol, sex, food, medication or some form of entertainment or escape. However, the moment the flame of love touches your heart, it changes everything. It is like giving you a taste of luxurious living. Even a small glimpse of the deep abiding love-peace-bliss of this "flame of love" is much more deeply fulfilling than anything of this world. When you spend even a moment there, it will be painful to leave your rediscovered home and return to something that you once considered normal. If you were made to come back, you would sense the change immediately. If you harbored unloving or judgmental thoughts about anyone or in response to any situation, you would clearly sense your heart close and experience the heavy transition into suffering. This is all because a new sense or awareness has been awakened in you. This awakened awareness, called *Prajna,* is the light that emanates from the flame of love. It is the homing instinct that guides you back to your natural state of love. It warns you whenever you slip back into a non-loving state, a foreign territory away from home.

Until the flame of love is lit in one's heart, one may not even know that one is suffering in spite of being deeply entrenched in it; or one may simply be in denial of the suffering. Unaware of the enormity of your own suffering, you may be also be unaware that you are inflicting it upon others. Even if you do sense the suffering within, you may not be aware of how to come out of it or how to stop inflicting it on others. You may blame it on the world, the human race, your upbringing, on "God," or maybe on fate or "bad luck."

You may have little power over the outside world, but you always have a free choice as to how you wish to feel in the world inside of you. When you believe that how you are going to feel within is dependent on what happens (or has happened) outside of you, you give up this freedom. You give the remote control of your life to the world around you. Somebody presses a button, you become angry; someone presses a button, you are flattered. At times we are happy, at times we are sad; and we imagine this must have something to do with our external affairs. Thus we live, constantly moving from one emotion to another, living at the mercy of the world. This is how I used to live until I was touched by the flame of love, when I experienced unconditional love inside of me even when nothing "exciting" was happening outside. These feelings of amazing grace would happen in such simple moments as: deep meditations, walks in nature, watching the sunset, in the company of sages, in simple acts of kindness, etc. The resulting feeling of fulfillment was far superior to any of the pleasures or thrills that came from satiating the physical, mental or egotistical desires I used to constantly strive and compete for earlier. It became clear that what I feel within me is completely independent of external situations. I still had the same job, I still had the same people around me, and I was still faced with the same challenging situations in life; but how I felt from within was a blossoming lotus flower untouched by the dirty pond on which it floated. Having experienced amazing bliss completely independent of my life situation, I felt the delusion that "other people and situations of the world were responsible for my happiness" begin to disappear.

The transformation was not instant. Whenever my mind responded to a situation or person with resistance (out of old habits) by entering a non-loving space, my heart would trigger suffering accompanied by unease, stress and heaviness. It was no longer easy to ignore the suffering resulting from stepping away from my true home of unconditional love. The difference between the two states was so great that it was hard to ignore or deny it. And since I was no longer under a delusion that other people or situations were responsible for my joy, I knew that the choice to remain in love or to step away from it was in my own hands. The little things that I used to strive and compete for were no longer as important as preserving the connection with the loving space, my true home. Nothing was more important than to be guided by this flame of love, which I knew would guide me back to the radiant light of the eternal sun within.

Take a break from your head space; take a break from the constant stream of thoughts that compare, judge, expect, criticize and worry about things. Spend time in your heart space around those who just live and love every moment. Spend some time in nature, around plants, around animals, around children (and if you are lucky, around awakened sages). Allow them to light the flame of love inside your heart. Once it is lit, spend some time with your Self in meditation, nurturing and growing this flame of love within. Allow yourself to be guided by *prajna*, the light that emanates from this flame. It will guide you back home, to the abode of infinite love.

# Chapter IX

## Love is the Greatest Teacher

"The Loving All Method can be summed up as follows: Love everything you perceive, exactly as it is. Love everything you experience, exactly the way it is."
- Chapter 12, Verse 5, "The Most Direct Means to Eternal Bliss" by Michael Langford

\*\*\*

As you sit and read these words, slow down and become aware of the loving space within you and around you; and lovingly allow all things to be exactly as they are. Feel the love flowing in your breath and in your veins. Allow it to embrace you from within and without.

You are perfect as you are, right here, right now.

No matter what situation you are in at this moment, love it.

No matter what state your body is in at this moment, love it.

No matter what emotion you are feeling at this moment, just love it.

Love everything that you perceive in the moment, with all your heart, all your might. I promise you, if you do this sincerely, it will bring a radical shift within you and draw you back to love no matter how distant it may have seemed to you a few moments ago.

Love is here, now. Allow it. Feel it.

***

Love is perfect harmony with "what is." When you bring love to whatever situation you are in, it opens up channels for more love to flow in. No matter how bitter the situation, love will bring sweetness into it; no matter how tense your body, love will bring ease into it; no matter how sorrowful your heart, love will bring joy into it; no matter how dark it seems, love will bring light into your soul.

Love is the greatest teacher. When there is love in your heart, like a guiding light, it will show you the way out of even the deepest, darkest alley back into open sunshine. When you have love on your side, be assured, you have all that you need to return to the ultimate place within - Supreme love itself.

In the past, whenever I felt a low emotion, I used to resist it. I used to have an attachment to "higher" loving emotions, or so I imagined. But whenever you have a preference for one over another, it is not true love; for in that preference for one is hidden a resistance to another. And wherever resistance is present, love is not. Whatever you resist persists; when I didn't know any better I would be stuck in the "lower" emotion for a while, even as I tried hard to resist it so that I could get back to a "higher" place. The more I tried to resist, the more it disconnected me from love and the "lower" I would go.

Now, if I sense a low emotion, I just love it. I surround it with love with all my heart without wishing any "negative" feeling to go away (You can either love something or wish it to go away; you cannot do both at the same time). When I do this sincerely, like an alchemical transformation, love eventually transforms the emotion back to love (although you should never expect this to happen, just allow it to happen if it does).

"When you are at unease with 'what is,' you experience suffering. When you are at ease with 'what is,' you experience peace. When you are in love with what is, you experience 'bliss.' Even if your present experience of 'what is' is that of pain, in the presence of love, that pain dissolves and what remains is pure love and joy. All your suffering starts to dissolve as you let go of thoughts that are in resistance with 'what is.' As you grow more and more at ease with 'what is,' you will notice that the suffering gets transformed into peace, and then into an ocean of bliss" - Yogi Kanna, *Nirvana: Absolute Freedom*

In the past, when people shared their problems with me, I used to give them advice. I thought my advice would help them. It only made them more confused.

Imagine there is a treasure inside a big house, but it is very dark inside with no windows or lights. At the entrance to the house, is stationed a security guard. He gives you a choice: Either you can take inside the house a detailed instruction map which shows you how to navigate through the house, or you can take with you a bright lamp. You can choose only one of the two. Which one would you choose?

Choosing the bright lamp is the wiser thing to do, isn't it? What use is a detailed map of the house when you cannot even see it or anything else in the darkness? When you choose light, it may not be instantly clear where the final treasure is, but it lets you see where you are. By choosing light, you can find your own way around the house. It keeps you from stumbling over objects; it helps you navigate the maze-like rooms, and eventually, as you keep looking, the light will guide you to the ultimate treasure inside the house.

Similarly, when people are in deep suffering, seldom is it useful to give them words of advice. Words of advice given to those in suffering are like giving directions to a person trapped inside a dark house.

They are likely to misinterpret the directions and stumble over things and lose their way. I realized that it is much more valuable to simply give love to someone when they share their problems with me. Love, like a guiding light, gives the person exactly what they need: the ability to see and guide themselves.

However, you can give love to others only when you have access to love within your own heart, as the master in the following story illustrates:

\*\*\*

A disciple asked his spiritual teacher: "Master, I have been meditating sincerely two hours a day every day for the last five years. I have found great peace inside myself. Please tell me what I can do to help others to find this peace within themselves?"

The master replied, "If you would like to be of use to others, then increase your own meditation to four hours a day instead of two hours a day."

The disciple said, "But master, how would increasing my meditation help other people? I don't understand."

"Son, Love is the greatest wealth. When you are in touch with this wealth within yourself through meditation, you are established in a state of self-contentment. When you are self-content from within, you can be at perfect ease with whatever happens on the outside; this gives you the ability to love everyone as they are without trying to change anything about them. This is the biggest gift you can give others."

"I see," replied the disciple.

"Just as you cannot help the poor when you are poor yourself, it is not possible to love when you yourself feel alienated from love." said the master. "When you are disconnected from your heart, love simply remains as a concept in your head. Daily meditation gives you a glimpse into the wealth of love that lies buried deep inside your heart. This wealth is often forgotten when we get caught up in the things of the world. And when we forget what we have, it is like not having it at all. And when you forget your own wealth, you become needy and try to get happiness by stealing it from others."

"Look at those wild buffaloes," said the master, directing the pupil's attention to a few that were resting in a ditch outside the sage's hut. "Why do you think they willingly subject themselves to the stench of dirty muddy water?"

He continued: "Unable to find access to clean waters, they rest in dirty muddy water in order to stay cool. They ignore the stench from the dirty water so that they can gain some solace and escape from the terrible heat of the sun. Similarly, when you don't have access to the place of pure love within, you may even engage in self-destructive and unloving habits just to get some temporary relief from the heat of suffering. Disconnection from the place of love is the beginning of all evil. Constant remembrance of the love within and constant experience of the love within through daily meditation is the best way to share the love with others. Even if you don't do or say anything, simply remaining in touch with this love will be of great help to others. However, when you are disconnected from love, no matter what you do to help others, it will cause chaos and confusion."

"Spending more time in meditation in communion with the infinite love within will help you cultivate a stronger connection to that source," said the master, "Once you have a strong connection to this huge reservoir within, the love will keep you grounded during interactions with other people. When you embody love, nothing is unacceptable and you can remain as a silent witness, radiating love to the other person without resisting them in any way through your words or actions. When they receive this gift as a result of your rootedness in love, it will light the flame of love inside their heart. That flame of love will do the needful and teach them what they need to learn. You don't need to do anything. You simply need to strengthen your own connection with love through daily meditation."

The disciple nodded in agreement.

\*\*\*

When people share their suffering with you, your body starts vibrating at the same frequency as that of the other person. We have been gifted with this human body so that we can empathize with others and share each other's feelings at a relational level. In the past, I completely misused this gift. When someone shared their story, and I began to feel their suffering, since I was not grounded in the reservoir of love within myself through daily meditation, I would grow uncomfortable and resistant to the emotions of others. I would either want to solve the other person's problem so that I could feel better within myself, or I would want to walk away. In my well-meaning empathy, I would put myself in their shoes and start giving them advice on how to get out of the situation. However, as we saw in the example of the dark house and the map, such advice is useless. It made the person more confused, and it would make me feel even more uncomfortable. Even after the meeting would be over, the emotional charge would linger within me for a while. And if I resisted this feeling, it would take even firmer hold of me.

Over the years, I have realized that a much better way to listen to someone is by staying connected to the love within; when you do this, it reflects in your body as a feeling of ease, joy and peace within. By using these feelings as a gauge I can tell whether I am grounded in love or if am slipping into a non-loving space. By staying aware of what is happening in your body, you can sense whether you are staying connected with love or getting pulled into the emotions and thoughts of the other person.

Now, as I listen to others, I ground my attention into my body, feeling the feet touching the ground connecting all the way up to my crown, feeling the freedom in my neck, the head balanced at the top of the spine, the arms hanging at the shoulders on the sides of the torso, etc. The more conscious I become, the more I can let go of any unnecessary tension within. [For more information on body awareness and the way to use yourself consciously, learn about the Alexander Technique by reading the book "*Use of the*

*Self*" by F.M. Alexander]. When I listen from a state of inner-connectedness, I immediately notice any changes within me. Our bodies are designed to mirror the feelings of the other person. The muscles in our body and the thoughts in our mind tense and relax in a reflection of the other person we connect to; as I listen, if I notice any tension beginning to build up in my muscles or thoughts, I surround it with love and like a free flowing stream, the love will melt away any excess tension or effort and put my body back in touch with a feeling of ease, peace and joy. When I resist nothing, things flow easily through me without sticking. I am able to feel the emotion of the other person, but yet remain unaffected by it, as I keep releasing it and returning back to love, returning back to the ease, peace, and joy within. I have noticed that when you stay connected with this loving ease within yourself, slowly the other person's being will start vibrating on the same frequency as yours and they themselves will start to shift from a state of tension and stiffness into a state of ease and fluidity. They may sense a calm descend over them.

When you listen from a place of love, you give others a gift of love. Even without a single word spoken through you, they will have received a valuable lesson. When they are able to connect to this love, it will immediately remind them whenever they slip back into suffering. When you have a light in your hand, it will show you if there is a steep staircase in front of you and help you avoid stumbling over it. Similarly, when you have love in your heart, it will immediately show you whether your actions lead you to a place of deeper love or toward suffering. Without love, perceptions can become distorted, and people may end up engaging in activities they imagine will bring pleasure while they really result in pain. So instead of giving people advice and directions, I have noticed that simply giving love is much more effective.

Giving love opens channels of communication to the hearts of others. After a loving connection is felt, if a few words are said, they make it through very easily to the other person. Any advice given prematurely before a proper heart connection is established through love is loaded with risk. You may come across as arrogant and disrespectful. Pointing out flaws to someone trapped in sorrow is a recipe for disaster. Just as someone drunk with alcohol will be unable to perceive logic or reason, a person drunk with emotion lacks the ability to receive critical feedback. When you keep radiating love, eventually the emotions will heal and the light of love will show them all their flaws without you having to open your mouth even once. You may even find them opening up about their own flaws, and laughing at their earlier folly which caused them to blame someone or something else for their perceived suffering. Opening ourselves to love for even a brief moment can teach us things that we could never learn from years of listening to lectures or reading books. Indeed, Love is the greatest teacher.

Q. Do you always listen from a place of love?

A. No. I often forget, but if and when I do slip into a non-loving place, my heart immediately senses it and warns me, "Watch out dear, you are losing your way from love, your true home." When I notice this, I forgive myself, and surround myself with love. By inviting love into the moment, I can get myself up again and let it guide me back to even more love.

When you have love by your side, you always win. Love has the power to bring light to the darkest of situations.

# Chapter X

## Meditation and the Art of Returning to Love

Each moment is unique, just like every breath of yours is unique. Notice your breath now. Notice how an old breath leaves, and notice how a fresh breath comes in and fills up your lungs. When you allow this natural flow of breathing to continue, life continues. Breathing doesn't require any effort, nor does meditation.

To meditate is to be in a state of free flow with life, letting go of and releasing each moment that just passed and opening your heart fully to the "is-ness" of "this" new moment. Just as you have to empty your lungs of old air to take in a full breath of fresh air, meditation involves letting go of the past moment or an imagined future moment completely so that you can be fully open and available to draw in the fullness of this present moment. When you allow this natural flow to continue, you abide in your true state of Love, the true source of abundant joy and peace.

Imagine that you are walking through a rose garden, and as you take a breath in, the scent of the roses fills you with a pleasant sensation. But just because the breath was so pleasant, will you now bottle up that air inside your body by pinching your nose? If you do so, you will choke yourself to discomfort if not to death. Even though you have now passed through the garden, it is time to let out the old breath and time to take in a fresh breath. If you hold on to a past breath just because it was pleasant, and resist the new breath just because it isn't as sweet to smell, you will cut yourself off from experiencing life.

Similarly, Life happens in a flow. New moments follow old ones. When you are in a state of free flow, constantly embracing the "is-ness" of life, you are in touch with pure love, the very essence of life. No matter what shape or form this present moment takes, the love that you are connected to will fulfill you. In that state of connectedness with love, you can play with the things of this life that come and go without taking them too seriously.

However, when you attempt to hold on to a moment and bottle it up with a thought that this is what life "should be" like, or oppose a moment by saying, life "shouldn't be" like this, it disconnects you from love, disconnects you from life, and puts you in a state of suffocation and suffering.

The moment you fall into your head space and become one with a thought, it disconnects you from your heart space, separating you from love. During the day, stop every now and then and notice if you are living in your heart space loving, and releasing every moment; or are you living in your head space, judging and resisting every moment.

Take enough time every day to sit down quietly and reconnect with the essence of your true being.

Try it now.

As you read these words, slow down and gently bring attention to this moment.

Sit or lie down in a comfortable position.

Notice that you are supported. Let go of any excess tension in your body and let your support carry your weight.

Become a loving space and radiate love to every particle of your being, within and without.

Let all things be exactly as they are.

Love doesn't attempt to change. Love simply loves, and in that love everything melts into love.

Notice your breath. Let go of any effort to control or hold your breath, and allow it to flow freely without any resistance.

Love doesn't hold, love just flows.

Become the loving space that allows the free flow of the is-ness of this moment.

Emotions appear and disappear, just as clouds appear and disappear in the sky. Be like the open sky, allowing the emotions to be exactly as they are.

Just notice the space around them and abide as a loving space that allows emotions and feelings to appear and disappear.

Thoughts appear and disappear, just like waves on the ocean. Be like the ocean of love, releasing every thought to the shore as soon as they appear.

Be the loving space that constantly releases and empties itself of the past moment, and fully opens itself to embrace the present moment.

Neither resist anything that appears, nor hold on to anything that is to disappear.

Just love, love and love everything, as it appears and as it disappears.

Greet every moment with love, showering everything that enters your heart space with love.

Don't complete thoughts, lest they should dislodge you out of your heart that loves into your head that judges; if you ever notice that you are slipping from the heart into the head, from "being" into "doing," just notice it and keep coming back to love.

The process of constantly returning to love is called Meditation. When you abide in love effortlessly, it is Realization.

"Keep empty, keep available, resist not what comes uninvited. In the end you reach a state of non-grasping, of joyful non-attachment, of inner ease and freedom, indescribable, yet wonderfully real." - Nisargadatta Maharaj

# Chapter XI

## Prayer for Love

A man approached a sage and asked "Sir, I am in a lot of suffering. I don't know how to come out of it."

"Try Meditation son," said the sage.

"But sir, my mind is not interested in meditation. I can't sit still for even two minutes," said the man.

"Then try Prayer," replied the sage.

"But sir. I don't believe in prayer."

"Ok my child. Then just continue to suffer."

*** 

Your true Self is an ocean of endless love. If at any moment you feel disconnected from love, simply pray for it with a sincere heart and invite the abundance of love to fill your being.

Your heart is both a transmitter and a receiver of love. The easiest way to switch on the receiver of love in your heart is by beginning to transmit love. The heart referred to here is your spiritual heart, not your physical one. Some find it helpful to feel the spiritual heart around the spot 2 inches to the right hand side of your chest center, unlike the physical heart which is located directly in the center (Many erroneously think that the physical heart is located on the left side of the chest. If you look up pictures of human anatomy, you will find that the human heart is really in the middle of the chest between the right and left lung although slightly tilted to the left).

Try this now. Start radiating love to your true Self within your heart and feel that love grow in you as you silently read the sample prayer below. The love you radiate out to your Self will return to your heart magnified several times.

*Oh my true Self, You are an ocean of infinite love.*

*You are the true abode of my heart.*

*Please help me remember the highest love,*

*And lift my soul back to where I really belong.*

*Please shower me with your nectar of grace,*

*And melt all walls of separation from the loving space.*

When you invite love into your heart, there is no problem too big for love to handle. Like a beacon of light, it will show you the way out of darkness. Call out to your true Self and pray for love sincerely with an open heart.

Give love, receive love.

Let Love in. Keep praying, sending and receiving love and experience the Holy Communion with your true Self, the abode of infinite love.

Notice the stream of love trickle into your heart filling up every particle of your being. As you feel more love, start radiating even more love within and without. Receive even more love. Envelop everything and everyone that appears in your awareness with this love.

Stay connected with this stream of love.

Come back to it as often as you can. Read the chapter again slowly, and try praying with closed eyes. Feel your spiritual heart center, start radiating love to your true Self, and start receiving love. Try it for a minute today and gradually increase the length every day. Do this prayer any time of the day you are in need of love. Your heart will be thankful.

# Chapter XII

## The Process of Returning to Love

Whenever you feel like you're slipping away from a place of love or feel stuck in a place far removed from love, go through the steps outlined below to guide yourself back home.

The process of returning to love involves six steps:

I. ***Pratikraman*** – Slow down and stop the moment you slip into a non-loving space.

II. **Self-Love:** Surround your emotions with Self-love and non-judgment.

III. **Root Thought:** Trace the root-thought behind the emotion.

IV. **Preliminary inquiry and *Prati-Paksha Bhava*:** Perform preliminary inquiry and apply *Prati-paksha bhava* to release and let go of negative thoughts and to return to love.

V.    **Introspective Meditation (*Samayik*)**: Meditate to deeply inquire and resolve the root-thought that causes painful emotions.

VI.    **Penance (Tapas)** - Anchor yourself to the highest truth at the time of big challenges.

> **Step 1: Pratikraman** - Slow down and stop the moment you slip into a non-loving space.

The moment you experience a non-loving thought toward anyone or in response to any situation, prajna (the awakened awareness) should immediately warn you that you are entering a foreign territory and triggering a stressful feeling/emotion inside your heart. Remember, love is always accompanied by ease, lightness and joy. Whenever, you experience unease, heaviness or stress, it is your heart warning you: "Be careful my child, you are slipping away from Love, your true home."

Imagine that you are driving on a steep hill, you take a wrong turn, and there is a danger sign that reads: "Wrong Way – Steep Precipice Ahead!" What will you do?

The first step upon noticing the danger signal is to apply the brakes, slow down and STOP. This act of stopping immediately the moment you recognize you are straying away from your true home of love is called *Pratikraman*. [For more detailed information on *Pratikraman*, you can read the book of *Pratikraman* by Dadashri].

## Step 2: Self-Love - Surround your emotions with Self-love and non-judgment.

Remember that the process of slowing down and stopping (*pratikraman*) upon sensing a painful emotion in the previous step is not an act of suppression or control; quite the contrary. Suppressing emotions on the inside while pretending to be fine on the outside is like boiling water in a pressure cooker with the steam release valve closed. This may lead to a fatal explosion! The build-up of steam can be stopped only by putting out the fire that's causing the water to boil, not by closing the valve. Similarly, emotions are not to be controlled or suppressed; instead, we have to address the root cause (the fire of thoughts) that's causing the steam of emotions to build up. Emotions are simply the effect; the cause lies in the thought. By addressing the cause, the effect is taken care of. When we release the negative thoughts (put out the fire), the negative emotions (steam pressure) will gradually subside and transform back into love.

Often non-loving thoughts like judgments, jealousy, suspicion, etc., happen so fast that before we realize it, they cause us to boil from within and build up a storm of emotion and hurt. Slowing down and stopping allows us to trace the non-loving thought that's causing this emotion. By pausing, we can look at this thought (the cause behind the emotion) and see if the direction in which it is urging us toward is really an appropriate one. Stopping allows us the opportunity to conduct a simple inquiry in order to remember the truth about the higher choice and return from the state of low emotion back to our natural state of love.

Before inquiry however, the important thing is to surround the emotion with love. Negative emotions are like crying babies. When a child is in a crying fit, if you scold the child "Stop crying. Why are you crying? Quiet down and tell me what happened," do you think the child will co-operate? She will start crying even louder, won't she? However, if you embrace the child lovingly and say, "Oh my dear. It's okay, it okay. I love you," she will calm down and become responsive. When she calms down, you can ask her "What happened my dear?" She is more likely to cooperate and tell you what's going on, isn't she? Similarly, your own emotions respond better to inquiry when you pause and shower self-love, instead of showing displeasure or self-criticism. Criticism like: "I shouldn't be feeling this emotion. Why am I feeling this nasty emotion?" will only cause you to feel more guilty about the emotion and make it even worse. So before inquiry, just embrace the emotion with the warmth of love and become a loving space that allows the emotions to be exactly as they are. Visualize yourself as a space of loving consciousness. Notice the space in which these emotions and feelings arise. Don't try to change them or get rid of them. Become the loving space that allows them to be. Let go and relax into the space [You can do the Guided

Meditation Practice taught at the end of this book, an audio track of which is also available from the website www.yogikanna.com.] The topic of Self-love is discussed in much more detail in chapter IX, "Love is the Greatest Teacher" and Chapter XIII, "The Healing River of Love." Also look up chapter XI, "Prayer for Love" if you find it difficult to feel love in the presence of painful emotions.

## Step 3: Root Thought - Trace the root thought behind the emotion.

After you bring yourself to a pause (*Pratikraman*) and surround the emotions/feelings with love, gently ask yourself: what is the thought that's bothering me and causing this lower emotion or suffering?

As we have already seen, Love is perfect harmony with "what is" while suffering is intense unease with "what is."

The "what is," the present moment can take any shape or form. Love is to be in a state of free-flow embracing and opening up to the fullness of the moment exactly the way it presents itself. However, if you have any strong preference for what shape the present moment or the future moment should take, immediately it creates two possibilities "Right" and "Wrong." When "what is" is in alignment with your preference, it is "Right," when "what is" is out of alignment with your preference it is "Wrong." The moment you identify with a thought that has a preference in opposition to "what is" and are perceiving the moment to be "Wrong," immediately you will find yourself slipping from the lightness and ease of love, into the unease and stress of suffering.

Lower emotions are always caused by some form of resistance or non-loving thoughts that seek to "Right" the "Wrong." Even if you don't have any active situation or person that your mind is considering "Wrong," then your suffering could simply be the result of holding on to a thought as simple as "I don't like this emotion or feeling; it is wrong for me to feel this way. I want to feel different." What you resist persists. The previous step of surrounding the emotion with love [which is explained in more detail in the chapters "Love is the Greatest Teacher" and "The Healing River of Love"] will automatically put you in the right direction for those kinds of thoughts. However, in case you perceive thoughts of someone or something that is "Wrong" in connection with these negative emotions, try to find out what those thoughts are:

Various forms of thoughts which seek to correct the "Wrong" and the emotions they cause are given below:

- Thoughts that seek to change the past (resentment and guilt)
- Thoughts that seek to change the present (resistance to active physical, emotional or psychological pain, anger, failure/rejection, disappointment, loneliness, depression, lack of self-worth, lack of freedom, etc.)
- Thoughts that seek to control the future (fear, anxiety, worry)
- Thoughts that seek a different present (longing for something you don't have: craving/lust, jealousy, envy, boredom)

- Thoughts that seek to hold on to a past which is no longer present (attachment to something pleasurable that is no longer in your life: grief)

- Thoughts that seek to hold on to the present (afraid of losing what you have: greed and fear)

Thus, suffering is a state of identification with a thought or a set of thoughts that are in conflict with "what is." When thoughts label something or someone in the present moment, a past moment or an imagined future moment as "wrong" and strive to get to or hold onto an idea of "right," it creates disharmony within and you experience suffering. You want to get to the "right," but you are stuck in the "wrong"; or you want to hold onto the "right" because you are afraid that it will go "wrong." This disharmony with "what is" and labeling it as "wrong" separates you from love, your true nature. This is the root cause of slipping away from one's natural state of ease, lightness and joy into a state of unease, heaviness and suffering.

**Step 4: Perform <u>preliminary inquiry</u> and apply _<u>Prati-paksha bhava</u>_ to release negative thoughts and to return to love.**

Once you identify the root thought behind a painful emotion, follow it up with an inquiry and ask yourself: "Is there any valid action that I can take to resolve this thought?" If there is any reasonable action that you can take in the present to address this thought, please do so lovingly, without losing your equanimity. However, if there is nothing you can do to improve the situation right at this moment; or if the available options are at the expense of losing your connection with love, follow it up with another inquiry: "What is more important: To be Love or to be Right?"

Ask yourself sincerely: "Is the precious natural state of abiding in perfect love worth losing in favor of arguing or worrying over petty things? Is it worth insisting on having it my way in the external world when it leads to the loss of internal peace and equanimity?"

Imagine you are a millionaire walking down the street and a quarter accidentally falls out of your pocket. A guy picks up the quarter and claims it as his. Two shady-looking fellows come and tell you, "This guy is wrong in claiming your quarter. You should confront him and demand it back." A wise old man watching from the side of the street says, "Sir, you look like a wealthy person. Why waste your time and energy fighting over a trivial quarter. Just forget about it and move on. Maybe you can give a dollar bill to each of these people and spread some happiness with your generosity. You will still have a lot of wealth left when you return home. Why fight over a quarter?" Would you listen to the shady guys and get into a fight or would you listen to the wise old man? If you listen to the shady guys and confront the man who picked up the quarter, you may be risking your life, all for a petty quarter. Is this risk worth taking? The wise thing to do would be to politely excuse yourself from the situation as the old man suggested. Similarly, when you encounter non-loving thoughts (the shady guys) that urge you to go on the offensive, think twice and reflect on whether it's worth taking that risk. Listen to *prajna*, the awakened awareness (wise man) that warns you to return to love. Remember your treasured property, love, and let go and forgive and return to the place of true fulfillment. If you fall for the prodding of the negative thoughts (shady guys), the spiritual loss that you incur, moving into lower emotions and losing touch with the loving space, will be much greater than the petty gain you may get from proving your point by listening to those thoughts.

"Why clash with one who willingly chooses a self-destructive path? Such a person will never attain liberation and will impede your liberation. Avoid engaging your intellect with such people. Be very cautious in such instances. Make a smooth exit without creating friction. If the train for your liberation is about to depart from the platform and your loincloth is caught up in a barbed wire, in this situation do not wait to disentangle your loincloth. Let it remain behind, run and make sure that you do not miss the train. It is not worth getting stuck in any worldly situation, even for a moment. In any situations where you get caught up in worldly interaction you forget the Self." – *Dadashri*

The energy you feed into thoughts has great power. It results in emotions that radiate to your heart and from there to everyone around you. All of us may seem like discrete people separated physically by space and time. However, we are all deeply connected with one another emotionally as well as spiritually. The moment you have a negative thought about anyone and think them to be wrong, the vibration from the resulting negative emotion reaches them instantly no matter how far they are separated from you in space and time. Eventually these thoughts and feelings get reflected back to you. Remembering this, give only what you would like to receive yourself. For all of us, love is our true home; it is what our heart truly cherishes. So seek to give love always. Even if you feel someone has wronged you, be quick to forgive and quickly return to love. As Jesus said, "Forgive them for they know not what they do." Notice that straying away from love is a huge loss. As soon as any negative thoughts arise, just allow them to appear in your space of love and release them by not giving them any energy. Thoughts are not personal, so don't criticize yourself for having them; just notice them arising and keep releasing them. Direct the mind to notice the positive things in the current situation that help bring you to back the feeling of love. The mind is like an ant: if you put a finger in front of it, it will stop and move in a different direction; if you put a finger in front of it again it will move in yet another direction. When you task your mind to find fault with somebody or some situation, it will keep digging into the negative and create terrible emotional pain in you. Simply redirect the mind to think about the positive things in your life. Ask your mind: "Tell me three positive things in this situation." Replace pessimism with optimism, suspicion with benefit of the doubt. This will shift your mind into the direction of love. When you bring love to your heart, your mind may even notice certain positive things about the same person or situation it was generating non-loving thoughts about earlier.

There is nothing you can do about a present negative emotion you feel; emotions are simply the result of holding onto negative thoughts. Just as a laptop computer battery starts losing its charge after you leave it unplugged, emotional charge will start dissipating as soon as you leave your mind unplugged from negative thoughts. As soon as you release the negative thoughts and return to love, bringing love around your emotions, you will notice that the negative emotions gradually transform back into love. Staying rooted in love will cause your heart to radiate loving feelings to anyone who appears in your awareness. It will all get reflected back to you and strengthen your own connection with love. This process of making the higher choice of love and transforming negative feelings into positive ones by changing the direction of your thoughts is called *Prati paksha bhava*. With practice, you will become an expert at catching even the minutest deviation from the loving space: the slightest irritation in thoughts, the minutest change in the tone of your voice, the slightest onset of jealousy or ill will in your intent. The better you become at catching even the smallest slip from your true abode of pure love, the closer you are to liberation.

Remember, this choice of love happens within. At no point is it suggested that you should tolerate abuse or put up with any action that you feel is inappropriate. If you find yourself in a situation or with a person you find untenable, feel free to remove yourself from the situation if you need to. What's being suggested is that you do so lovingly without disturbing your own inner peace. Gently close the door behind you instead of slamming it shut. Be assertive but not aggressive. Love it that it didn't work out, and love it that you need to move on. If a few words came out of your mouth in the heat of the moment, just start over from the beginning: Surround the emotion you feel with self-love, trace the root thought, inquire if holding onto the thought brings you closer to love or takes you away from it, release and let go, return to love - and lovingly move on to wherever love leads you. Love doesn't mean inaction. Love means to keep flowing wherever love leads you, and to completely let go of things that draw you away from love.

Traversing the world in the absence of love is like roaming around in a dark house: you might trip and fall on the most benign things and curse them as obstacles. When you return to love, the light turns on inside your soul and enables you to find a way through even the biggest obstacles.

Questioner: "You say that one should not steal or do violence. But if a person steals from us or cheats us, should we confront him or not?"

Dadashri: "You have to confront him. Do it in such a way that it does not affect your peace within. Very calmly and deliberately ask, 'Brother, what wrong have I done that you are stealing and hurting me?' If he has stolen something worth a hundred rupees do not confront him with anger. If you do, you would have sustained a loss of five hundred rupees. You will incur a greater [Spiritual] loss by becoming angry with him."

## Step 5: Introspective Meditation (*Samayik*) - Meditate to deeply inquire and resolve the root thought that causes painful emotions.

Sometimes thoughts and emotions will be accompanied by a strong sense of righteousness and attachment, and you may find *Prati-paksha bhava* (releasing negative thoughts and returning to a space of love) to be quite difficult.

If the preliminary inquiry, "What is more important, being love or being right?" fails to bring clarity or equanimity, you can do an even deeper inquiry through a process called Introspective meditation or *Samayik* [the last 50 pages in the book of *Pratikraman* by *Dadashri* explain this in much greater detail].

During *Samayik* or Introspective meditation, you may inquire: "What is so special about these thoughts that I am willing to risk abandoning the precious loving space and enter a place of suffering?" This gives you an opportunity to look at the consequences of believing the thoughts that urge you to enter a non-loving space and keep you trapped in worry or bitterness.

Try to see in minute detail the consequences of holding onto the thought that's causing the present suffering:

- Are there any strong preferences, expectations or likes/dislikes that are causing this situation or person to appear so "Wrong"?

- These strong preferences you have, are they worth holding onto at the cost of entering a world of suffering?

- According to your thoughts, what are the things that need to change about the situation or person to make you feel alright?

- Is there a peaceful way to bring about a resolution? What are the things the thought would like you to do to make it right?

- What happens when you hold on to the thought and insist on your viewpoint even if it causes disharmony with others? Does it cause more stress, or does it help you feel better?

- What are the things you do, the things you say, and the resulting feelings and emotions in yourself and in others?

- Do such words and actions result in a feeling of ease/freedom/joy, or stress/unease and suffering?

- Do you recognize that you have the freedom to return to your natural state of love, ease, lightness and joy regardless of what happens? Do you voluntarily choose to give up the freedom?

- What is more important, being love or being right?

[Aside: You can even do a written *Samayik* (written introspective meditation) by writing down the thoughts and inquiring into them. An inquiry technique called "Four questions and turnaround" by Byron Katie is also a good way to inquire into on troublesome thoughts.]

When you can see for yourself that remaining in love, your true home, is much more freeing, in that clarity the troubling thoughts will lose power over you and leave you in peace and joyful acceptance. Just as removing from the fire stops the boiling of water inside a vessel, releasing negative thoughts stops the buildup of negative emotions and gradually restores peace and clarity. As you keep gaining more clarity, you will notice that you are able to stay in equanimity and loving acceptance even in situations which in the past used to torment or irritate you easily.

You have to use every instance of disturbance as an opportunity to question the underlying beliefs and thoughts that trigger negative emotions and cause you to lose equanimity. With practice, the frequency of things that make you upset and the intensity of the upset will get smaller and smaller. You will become very skillful at returning to love from a state of upset emotions; so skillful that a day will come when you can remain in undisturbed peace and bliss within, even in the midst of the biggest provocation or turmoil from outside.

A day will come when you can recall every single person or situation you have ever encountered, and not even the slightest trace of negativity will linger in you. Until then, your work is not done. Thenceforth, the resulting emotions you may experience from the thoughts that arise will be like tiny bubbles that appear on the surface of a river. They will disappear the moment they appear. The flow of love in your heart will be so strong, that anything that arises will get swept away by that river of love.

Note that as long as you have an ego that separates itself from others, you will always experience emotional resistance which comes from identifying with thoughts/preferences inside you that label things as "right" and "wrong." Some people imagine that as you approach mastery you will grow completely insensitive to external events and somehow become numb and lifeless, like a dead vegetable. However, the opposite is true. As you approach mastery, you become extremely sensitive to what happens; so sensitive that you will recognize thoughts or expectations the very instant they arise, and release them as soon as you sense a slip into a non-loving space. The true home of supreme love is so dear to you that you instantly release anything that urges you away from it. This process is so quick in a master that it may give the appearance of being completely unaffected by external events.

"Say you are going somewhere with someone by car. He tells you to get in the car and you do. A little later, if he tells you to get out of the car because someone else is coming instead, what would you do? Would you just sit there? Would you tell him you are not getting out? Or would you get out with equanimity? Then as you walk away, he calls you back. You would go back, would you not? And you would do so without a change of expression on your face, right? There is nothing in the mind, the face remains smiling as if nothing has happened, and this is the case while getting off also. Then he asks you to get out of the car again, and then invites you back again. So what have I said? If this happens nine times and your equanimity remains nine times over without any effect at all, then I will tell you have become 'Dada'!" – Dadashri

## Step 6: Tapas (Penance) - Anchor yourself to the highest truth at the time of big challenges.

At times, you may encounter extremely challenging situations or people who trigger a violent emotional storm inside of you. There may be other times when you feel "low" or "heavy" for no reason, even though you may be doing everything "right." It is extremely important at these times to anchor yourself to the deepest truth that "Love is the greatest wealth" or you may lose yourself in a sea of suffering, carried by the strong winds of negative thoughts.

Understanding the nature of these challenges and how they came into being can be helpful in dealing with them. Sometimes when you find it extremely challenging to let go of a negative thought that keeps you stuck in negative emotion, in spite of knowing that love is your home you'd like to return to, the reason may be past karma. Past karma is seeds that you may have sown and watered in an earlier state of ignorance of your highest truth, the bitter fruit of which you have to face today.

For example, imagine you had a habit of smoking cigarettes, and you indulged in it by smoking one pack every day. Slowly you realized that smoking cigarettes is injurious to health and you no longer enjoyed the good health and energy you used to have before you started smoking. With this understanding, you quit; you no longer wish to smoke cigarettes. However, because of your past habit of smoking one pack a day, the addictive properties of cigarettes and the accompanying belief that it was pleasurable, you will be faced with withdrawal symptoms.

Withdrawal symptoms are like bitter fruits that have come from planting and watering seeds which at the time of sowing, you had no idea what they would grow into. Although today you recognize that these fruits are bitter, you nevertheless have to deal with them. With your new understanding, when you stop watering the tree it will stop producing more fruit and leave you in peace. You can plant new good seeds and enjoy good fruits in the future. However, until then, you have to eat the fruits that have come as a result of past watering of seeds.

Similarly, it is the past belief "I like smoking" that creates strong emotional urges (fruit of watering the wrong type of seeds) in you. For a few months or a year, you may get strong urges to smoke whenever you run into your old companions with whom you enjoyed smoking. These urges will become weaker and weaker with the passage of time as your new belief "I am better off without it" takes root and you stop watering the old tree (the belief that "smoking is good"). Some fruits can taste sweet for a second but leave a bad after-taste in your mouth. So don't impulsively water the tree fooled by the initial sweetness, or you will be left to deal with a lot of fruits that leave a bitter after-taste. Similarly recognize that the promise of momentary pleasure comes with the huge risk of relapsing into a destructive habit that propagates suffering. With this understanding you can stay rooted in your decision to choose long-term health over urges for momentary pleasure, and deal with the withdrawal symptoms by redirecting your attention to healthier habits. If you remain steadfast in your decision, the withdrawal symptoms will pass and you will emerge a winner, with a clear understanding of the consequences of the seeds you sowed in ignorance.

Just like with the smoking habit, we developed a "thinking/judging" habit, where we constantly encouraged non-loving thoughts and judged situations and people as "right" or "wrong"; we resisted and complained about the "wrong" and applauded and "welcomed" the "right."

One day you wake up and recognize that the fruits of the seeds you watered (non-loving thoughts) are not as sweet as you thought they would be. You decide that you no longer want to encourage thoughts of expectations, judgment, resistance, holding-on, suspicion, etc., as they lead you away from love, create terrible emotions in your body and radiate suffering within you and on to your family and everyone around you. However, you find these thoughts keep coming up in spite of your desire for them to stop.

At one time you had encouraged such thoughts and behavior, thinking they were helpful, and hence they gained energy. You strongly believed that having things a certain way or having certain people or things in your life were important for your happiness. But now you recognize that these very things lead you away from the unconditional love that flows with "what is" and keep you from your natural joy of being. You recognize that a time has come to let go of that habit of getting carried away by thoughts that dictate how things or people "should be," "could be," etc. But how do you stop when the force is so strong? Again, suppressing these thoughts or trying to escape from them with a different addiction (food, sex, alcohol, drugs, etc.) is not the solution. You will merely be replacing one problem with another. Patience and perseverance are needed to redirect the energy from a path to self-destruction into a path of love.

When negative thoughts or low emotions come along inviting you to leave your home of love, just recognize them as withdrawal symptoms from the habits of the past. Don't be discouraged by them or take them personally. Instead of budging from your place of love, invite them over by surrounding them with love! Stay rooted in love and let go of any thoughts that invite you outside of love. Remember, love neither resists nor holds onto anything; love just keeps flowing with what appears.

No matter how strongly and violently these storms brew from within, patiently anchor yourself to your highest truth, and the storms will surely pass. The process of holding on to the highest truth without slipping away at the moment of challenge until the storm passes is called *Tapas* or Penance. The literal meaning of the Sanskrit root of the word *Tapas* translates to heat or burning. Whenever you experience withdrawal symptoms, just call it *Tapas*, and say "This *Tapas* is burning away my past karma, and is taking me to deeper peace. I love it."

"It is the penance of not allowing the state of the Self (Home department) to mix with the state of the non-Self (Foreign department). To remain steadfast in, 'these are circumstances of the non-Self; they are not Mine,' is penance. Such penance was done by *Gajsukumar* when he was in meditation of the pure Self. His father-in-law built a clay fire pit on his head and filled it with hot burning coals [the father-in-law was avenging *Gajusukumar's* abandonment of his daughter in order to follow his spiritual call]. He realized then, 'O ho ho! This father-in-law is helping me by tying a turban of moksha (liberation).' In such penance, with the meditation of pure Self, he went higher and higher, attained *Keval-Gnan* (absolute knowledge) and went to moksha (liberation)." - *Dadashri*

Inquiry (outlined earlier in the chapter) followed by Meditation (See the section on Guided Meditation) should be your number one choice of remedy during times of *Tapas* to help you return to Love. If meditation is difficult, try prayer (see Chapter XI, "Prayer for Love") and surround yourself with love. However, if you find that the negative charge is too strong and doesn't allow you to sit still, you may even resort to chanting *mantras*, doing some physical exercises or anything to redirect your energies in a healthy manner away from fueling the negative thoughts that torment you. You may even soak your body in a salt water bath (use 1 cup of non-iodized salt with 1 cup of Epsom salt in a bath of warm water) for 10 minutes or swim in the ocean for 20 minutes to help release the charge. Or go take a walk in nature. Just as a tree stops producing fruits once you cut off the water supply, the painful emotions will subside when you don't charge the negative thoughts with your attention. If necessary, physically remove yourself from the place (or away from the person) that triggers these thoughts and emotions to give yourself the space to come back to your true Self, the loving space within. If necessary, seek the company of pure-hearted saints or practitioners (who can lead you to saints or sages) and study spiritual books written by liberated sages to help motivate you and remind you of your highest truth until the difficult time passes. If you stay anchored to your truth, the storm will pass, and you will come back with a stronger understanding of and connection with your loving space. Once you rediscover the loving space within you, don't let go of it. Stay in touch with it through daily Meditation. Try not to repeat the mistakes of the past when you willingly slipped away from a place of pure love. Remember the past lessons, anchor yourself to this true wealth, and never let yourself get lost again. The moment you slip, just notice it and keep returning to love, your true home.

# Chapter XIII

---

## The Healing River of Love

Pain is not a problem; it's simply a call for attention.

When you touch a hot plate, physical pain arises, calling you to release your grip. As you let go of the hot plate and immerse your hand in cool water, pain subsides and healing commences.

Similarly, Emotional pain calls for your attention to let go of the judgmental thoughts in your head and return to the coolness of love in your heart.

***

How are you feeling now?

There are two ways to answer this:
one is with your heart; another is with your head.

The heart is capable of only one feeling: Love.
There exists no other feeling in the heart except love.

And when you feel love, there's an instant recognition and unmistakable joy; for joy is just another name for love; it's not a separate feeling.

If your answer to the initial question was "good" or "bad," you are answering it with your head.

The moment you reside in your head as a judgmental thought, you are disconnected from the love in your heart.

Once you disconnect from love,
there's instant recognition and unmistakable sorrow.

If you are feeling "bad" now,
drop the judgment and return to love.

Only "this moment" matters to the heart;
no matter what shape it takes, just love it.

Worry not about what was or what will be or how long; such thoughts belong to the heavy head.

Greet the present moment with love; and release the previous moment with love.

Sit comfortably, and notice your breath now.

Let go of all effort to control your breath in any way, and simply observe the cycle of breathing.

As you keep watching your breath, feel yourself immersed in a healing river of love.

With every in-breath, feel the love flowing into your lungs, and then into your blood stream to your heart and then from there to every cell in your body.

With every out-breath, let go completely of all your burdens into this feeling of love.

Breathe in love, breathe out love.

Keep flowing in this timeless stream of welcoming and releasing; and bathe in the cool currents of love.

Let the breathing take care of itself and feel the healing presence of love in every cell of your body.

Only this feeling of love is real; all other feelings are illusions created by false thinking.

The only real good feeling is Love,
but there's no need to call it "good."

The moment you call something "good," you invite
three vultures: greed, pride and fear;

They'll sweep you out of the heart space and in to the
head in no time.

So let go of both "good" and "bad,"
And simply abide as a stream of ever flowing love.

It will heal you inside out.

\*\*\*

Thoughts are not personal. Thoughts come and
Thoughts go, like waves appear in the ocean and
disappear into the shore.

Sometimes you may have kind thoughts. Love it.

Sometimes you may have unkind thoughts. Love that
too.

"But wait. Am I not supposed to have only loving thoughts and avoid non-loving thoughts?" you may ask.

Let's see. Unkind thoughts or non-loving thoughts are critical thoughts that label things as "good" or "bad," "right" or "wrong." When you just notice critical thoughts, and allow them to flow without making a problem out of them, you are instantly back in the heart space abiding as love.

Love neither approves, nor does it disapprove. Love just flows, neither resisting nor holding on to anything.

However, when you criticize the same thought and call it "good" or "bad," "right" or "wrong," you are still in the head space, residing in another critical thought. The moment you judge a thought and criticize yourself for having it, you are disconnected from love.

Just as peace is never the result of a war, inner harmony can never result from self-criticism.

Love never criticizes. Love only loves.

Be it good thoughts, be it bad thoughts, love doesn't have a problem with them.

The moment you notice that you are trapped in your head space, trapped in thoughts, just pause, love and return to your heart space.

Love is like an ocean.

Just as an ocean releases a wave to the shore immediately after it rises, be a loving presence that releases a thought immediately upon noticing it.

Release thoughts as soon as they appear. Release thoughts even before they appear, lest they should draw you out of your heart space that loves, into a head space that judges and criticizes.

Thoughts are not a problem. Disconnecting from love is the problem.

Wherever there is criticism, love is not.

Wherever there is love, there is no problem.

When you sense a problem with someone or something, invite love into the moment.

Flow with love, neither approving, nor disapproving anything.

Get carried away by a constant feeling of letting go, constantly noticing and releasing what appears. A beautiful flow unencumbered by anything.

Just as darkness cannot exist in the presence of light, no problem can survive in the presence of love.

Be without prejudice.

Be love now.

Your heart will thank you.

# Chapter XIV

## Misfortune is the Best Fortune

"Misfortune is the best fortune." - Yoga Vasistha

"Favorable situations are vitamins for the body; unfavorable situations are vitamins for the soul."
– Dadashri

\*\*\*

When things are favorable and everything's going well, the world feels like a cozy little place where the awareness (*Prajna*) goes to sleep and the ego flourishes. However, when things become unfavorable, it wakes up the awareness inside us. We cannot afford to hold on to the slightest bit of ego when people or things that lead to "misfortune" show up in our life, for if we do, we will get pummeled left and right. Misfortune is indeed the best fortune, for it forces us to evaluate ourselves and shed any excess ego that we might be carrying around. Just as a diamond cutter polishes all dirt and debris away from the surface of a diamond, some situations and people in our life keep grinding away all imperfections from within us until we revert to our natural state of perfect love. Be thankful for those diamond cutters when they arrive, for they are the one who will take you back home.

The author has been blessed with many diamond cutters in his life. Every time his ego would raise its head, some situation or person would show up in the author's life to weed out the ego and polish off any imperfections until the author returned back to love. A few such incidents are mentioned below:

## Incident # 1

It was the summer of 2005 and I was driving through a busy intersection on the roads of the San Francisco Bay Area, when I noticed that the traffic was much slower than usual. I noticed that there had been an accident. One car had crossed over from the opposite side at a strange angle and crashed into another car and both of them had been badly damaged. It seemed like the people in the cars had already been rushed to the hospital, and there was a crew inspecting the accident spot. "How could people get into accidents like this?" I thought. "Don't they pay attention to the road? I could never do such a thing." Well, so much for my conceit. I was soon to find out the answer.

In a few weeks, I was leaving home to meet with a spiritual gathering, when something flashed in my mind. I was told that there was going to be an accident, but no one was going to be injured. I debated inside the car what I should do about it. I decided to wait and meditate in the car for five minutes, imagining that waiting would somehow negate the possibility of any such thing from happening should there be any truth to this flash warning. Then I started driving cautiously, but soon forgot about the whole thing and resumed normal driving. Suddenly someone passed my car at a high speed and cut me off. I was really annoyed. I started driving faster to catch up with this person and "teach them a lesson." I noticed that their car started to slow down, and I used this as an opportunity to speed past them. Suddenly I realized why they had slowed down. The traffic signal in front of us had turned red. While my mind was obsessed with overtaking this other car, I had failed to notice the signal. I slammed on the brakes, but my car was moving too fast, and came to a screeching halt in the middle of the intersection. A car came from one side and I heard a crunching sound "CRASH." I was relieved that the air bags hadn't gone off and everything seemed okay. A young woman came out of the car that had crashed into me, rightly annoyed, waving her fingers at me: "You are the one at fault, you ran the red light!" I apologized to her, and admitted my fault. She called the police to register an accident report, and we waited until they arrived. The girl insisted that we should stay put at the exact location until the cops arrived. People passed around us in their cars in the middle of the intersection. They were probably thinking "How could someone drive like this and get into such a stupid accident?" I would have told them, "Trust me, you don't want to know!" We inspected the damage. Thankfully, there was just a minor tear in the girl's bumper and a bent fender with a broken headlight in mine. My insurance company fixed our cars, and I had learned an important lesson: "Judge not lest ye be judged."

A few years later, as I was leaving home to attend a meeting, I had a similar flash in my mind that indicated to me that there might be an accident that day. I didn't know if it was my mind playing games with me or if it was a real premonition. But this time I was wiser. I noticed the effect of the thought and saw how it induced fear, and drew me away from love. *Prajna* alerted me with a warning, and I duly acknowledged it. I applied the brakes of *Pratikraman* and released the negative thought. I told myself that there was going to be no such accident and everything was going to be ok. I reminded myself that I had several years of driving experience and there was nothing to worry about (*Pratipaksha bhava*: Changing the direction of mind in a positive direction). I thanked the thought for alerting me and used it as an opportunity to drive carefully and cheerfully, paying close attention to the road. There were two or three instances where some drivers cut me off on the freeway dangerously. I will never know whether it was a mere coincidence or a confirmation of the earlier "premonition." I just stayed calm and kept driving cheerfully. In the end, things turned out to be great that day and there was no accident at all!

## Incident # 2

Another time I was talking to a friend who mentioned an acquaintance of ours was having problems with alcohol. "How could someone be addicted to something like alcohol?" I thought. "It is obviously such an unhealthy habit. Why can't they simply quit?" I didn't have to wait long to discover the answer. A few nights later while my body was fast asleep, I dreamt that I was an alcoholic. I had a glass of whiskey in my hand and was drinking away. I was intensely aware of all my feelings and emotions as I was drinking. The people around me wanted me to stop, but I had no intention of doing so. In the dream, I knew exactly what an alcoholic felt like. I suddenly woke up, and realized that it was only a dream. I felt relieved. I thanked the universe for teaching me yet again, this time in a much safer way: "Judge not lest ye be judged."

## Incident # 3

Throughout my life, I have had the good fortune of having friends and people around me who are kind and sensitive. They would get upset whenever I uttered anything egotistical. At first I used to blame others for being overly sensitive and accused them of misinterpreting my "benign" statements. However, when a good friend of mine made it clear to me how badly hurt he was by one of my comments, I was forced to evaluate myself and look at why I said certain things. In this particular incident, I had gone out with a bunch of friends to eat. This particular friend was in a jubilant mood, and wanted a picture of all of us to be taken while we dined. He asked me, "Can we ask the waiter to take our picture?" I wasn't particularly keen on it. "I am not that into pictures," I said, probably in a smug tone, "But you can go ahead if you want." We did eventually have the waiter take a picture with my friend's camera, after I reluctantly agreed. But instead of playing along, I had an uninterested look on my face when the picture was taken. My friend didn't say anything then, but two days later I got an email from him saying how arrogant I was and pointing out my character flaws by citing several other past incidents where I had also hurt him. I called him to apologize for any misunderstanding, but it only made him more upset and angry. Sub-consciously I was still blaming him for being over-sensitive, and not taking full responsibility for the incident, and he probably sensed the insincerity in my apology and quite justifiably got more upset. I could feel his raw emotions and how badly my words had hurt him. I started to examine myself and ask, "Why do I say and do certain things?" It was only the beginning of a long and continued process of self-evaluation.

It took several such incidents and people to show up in my life before I realized that these seemingly benign things that I said or did served no useful purpose other than to aggrandize my own ego. Any subtle criticism or complaint, whether it was about somebody or something, was just an effort by my ego to make itself look bigger and better in the eyes of others. Many other "benign" comments were to show off my knowledge about various things to others.

Even if the discussion is about "spiritual" topics, anything spoken through the mouth is likely an effort by the ego to say, "Look at me. Look how much I know."

Topics of discussion chosen to show off your knowledge can hurt another badly even if you don't aim at criticizing anyone in particular. The person in front of you may have strong favorable or unfavorable opinions about the topic that is being discussed. If you were to say anything to trigger their discomfort, it might not take long before your words have caused irreparable damage.

The ego is very insecure and is constantly looking for validation from others. Love has no such needs. Love is full and content in itself. In my continuing education, I noticed that whenever I abandoned the heart space of love, and entered the head space of the ego, I left a space of contentment and entered a space of lack. Criticism, judgment and need for validation soon followed to fill up this void. I realized that anything spoken from this head space of lack had little or no ability to heal, but always came with a potential to inflict hurt.

I have been blessed all my life to have some wonderful, kind and sensitive people around me who would get really upset at my slightest deviation into head space or if I acted in a way totally contrary to my stated principles. They would grind my ego down until I abandoned association of any such egotistical thoughts or expectations in my head, and returned to my heart space of unconditional love. Eventually I developed enough awareness that even before the other person said anything, I knew instantly in my heart if my words or actions had hurt them even to the slightest extent.

Pujyashree Deepakbhai Desai, disciple of Dadashri, often says that there are five levels of awareness. They can be summarized as follows:

## Five Levels of Awareness

When you are at the first level, you will hurt others, but you won't even be aware that you have hurt anybody. When someone comes to you and says, "You have hurt me," you will defend yourself and deny it, and say something like: "Who, me? No way. You are the one at fault!"

When you are at the second level of awareness, you will still be unaware that you are hurting others. However, when someone brings it to your attention, you won't defend yourself. You will apologize and say, "I am really sorry. I didn't mean to hurt you. It won't happen again."

When you reach the third level of awareness, you will know the very instant that you hurt someone, even before anybody points it out to you. However, at this level, you won't be able to stop yourself from hurting others.

When you are at the fourth level of awareness, the *Prajna* will warn you from within before you can say or do anything to hurt others. Even before any hurtful word comes out of your mouth, you will have the awareness to stop. However, at this level, when other people say or do unkind things to you, you will get hurt, but you won't retaliate. You will be able to dissipate the upset emotions by returning to love.

At the fifth level, you will reach such a high state of awareness that no matter what anyone says or does, it won't upset you in the very least. You will experience and radiate constant bliss and love. You will make sure that every word that flows out of your mouth is true, kind and helpful.

What level are you at, dear reader?

***

Reflect on the diamond cutters in your life, the people and situations that have tested you. Feel grateful for them. They are the ones who can polish and remove even the slightest speck of imperfection from your heart if you will only allow them to. They will polish you until you become perfect shining diamonds. When they show up in your life, welcome them with open arms and say "Here comes another diamond cutter!" They are the ones who will take you back home, to true love. Once you return to love, you will see how pure they really are, and how big is the sacrifice they made. They have abandoned their heart space to teach you, so that you can return to yours. Your heart will overflow with gratitude.

Fear not misfortune; it is indeed the best fortune!

# Chapter XV

## Your True Love

The following story is adapted from a version in Agama Sutra as narrated by Gautama Buddha:

Once upon a time, there lived a king who ruled over a mighty dynasty. He won many battles, earned several titles, and was praised by many as one of the finest rulers of all. He had four beautiful wives whom he loved dearly.

One day he contracted a mysterious illness and his health started to fail steadily. He became bed-ridden and all the top doctors and healers of the kingdom failed to improve his condition. The chief doctor announced that they'd exhausted all possibilities and the king was truly counting his final days. The king became stricken with grief to leave everything behind and die with no one to accompany him. He felt dejected at the thought of loneliness. Then an idea struck him. He thought of his four beautiful queens who'd given him company and great pleasure during his life. Surely one of them could accompany him on this journey forward and offer him solace at this hour of need.

He first summoned his fourth wife. She was the king's favorite. She was extremely beautiful and he loved her dearly. He had always adorned her with the most expensive jewelry and the finest of garments; he served her rich cuisine and the finest wines; he took her to various exotic places for sight-seeing. He was very fond of her and had faithfully granted all her wishes.

"My dearest beloved," he said to his fourth queen, "you know how much I love you. I am at my deathbed counting my final days. Will you accompany me after death?"

"No," she cried, "That's impossible!" She left him in a hurry, leaving him devastated and heart broken.

The king gathered his strength and summoned his third wife. She was strikingly beautiful and the king took great pride in her. He showed her off to other kings, friends and relatives while entertaining them at parties and celebrations. He took great care of her and was very possessive of her. He loved her dearly and had even fought successful battles against other kings who'd attempted to take her away from him to make her their own.

"Oh my dear one," he said, "you know how much you mean to me. Will you come with me and accompany me in the after-life?"

"No, I cannot," she replied firmly. "In fact, I'm going to remarry after you're gone." So saying she left him there in complete shock.

Gathering himself and mustering some hope, he called for his second wife. She was very wise and compassionate, and the king had sought her counsel many times in the past. She'd offered him solace, comfort and encouragement at times of need and had been with him during bad times as well as good. Both had known each other for a long time and the king loved her dearly.

"Oh my dear," he said to his second wife, "You've been there for me through good times and bad. Surely, you'll give me company at this hour of need, won't you?"

His second wife was sympathetic. "Dear King. I care about you. But I cannot come with you after death. The most I can do is cry at your funeral and come to your grave. I'll miss you, but cannot come with you as I still have other things to attend to in this world. I am so sorry."

The king's heart sank in hopelessness. He felt dismayed. He started crying in silent agony, then called out, "Is there no one who loves me enough to come with me?"

"I will come with you!" He heard someone say in a sweet voice from across the room. It was his first wife. The king had completely forgotten about her. He had ignored her for a long time and she looked pale and weak from neglect.

"I will always be there for you, my king," said his first wife. "In fact, I have been there for you this entire time. Whenever you went into battles and came home tired and wounded, I applied medicines to your wounds and helped you heal as you slept on your bed. Whenever you were in need, I sent you help to rescue you from trouble. I have always been watching over you, and love you dearly. Even after death, I'll come with you. I will never leave your presence."

The king was overcome with guilt. "Oh my dear one," he said, "How foolish was I to have neglected you for so long. I always felt great joy in your company; but I forgot about you and wasted my time with others who were never my own. I wish I had given you the attention you truly deserved. You are my true companion, my true love." So saying, he embraced her. As he held her in loving communion, all boundaries dissolved and they merged into a shining light. There were no longer three separate entities: king, queen and the world. All appearances disappeared as in a dream, and a single self-aware being awoke in an ocean of infinite love that had aspects of both perfect stillness (masculine) and endless bliss (feminine), resulting in a timeless ecstasy of infinite-peace-bliss-love.

\*\*\*

The fourth wife in the story above represents your body; you have to leave it behind upon death. The third wife represents your wealth and possessions; someone else will inherit it upon death. The second wife in the story represents friends and relatives; they can cry at your funeral and come to your grave, but can go no further. The king in the story represents your spiritual heart, your awareness, which mistakenly assumes a false identity (ego) born out of attachment to temporary forms and thinks that it's going to die. But when you turn your attention within and rest it in the formless spirit represented by the first wife in the story, you realize that she's your true love; she's the one who's capable of giving you timeless fulfillment. Upon communion with her, you wake you from the nightmare of the ego and return to your true identity, your true Self: an ocean of endless love. You'll then rest in timeless contentment and never-ending bliss and peace.

How much time do you spend every day attending to your soul, your true love? She's the only one that truly matters. Everyone else including your own body will betray you. Turn within and enjoy communion with your true love. She'll wake you up to true life.

# Chapter XVI

## Love during Loss: An Aid to Sudden Awakening

Loss is often accompanied by an experience of suffering. The source of suffering is not the loss itself, but the attachment to the thing, person or experience that's lost. Imagine if your neighbor's son meets with an accident; you may feel some sympathy for him, but if it was your own child in his place, you'd feel severe anxiety or grief, wouldn't you? Similarly, when your neighbor's new car gets dinged, it doesn't bother you much; but a dent in your own brand new car can put a dent in your heart. Why is that? It's the presence of the thought "mine" that ties your heart up with strings of attachment. A loss pulls on this cord of attachment (and eventually snaps it) causing pain in your heart. The stronger the attachment, the greater is the pain when the object of attachment passes away. When you identify yourself with the place where all these strings bind to your heart, a false identity "I" is born out of attachment to various temporary forms it calls "mine." Your true identity is formless spirit, whose nature is love. It's the only thing that remains with you forever. As we have seen, Love doesn't get attached to anything; it just flows with "what is." Flowing with love and voluntarily letting go of things that pass allows you to rest in timeless contentment and frees you from the heartache that otherwise follows a loss. But when you forget your true identity as loving spirit, and tie your heart to temporary forms of this world with the thought "mine," you subject yourself to unnecessary torment as you witness these things parting from you one by one, as they inevitably will.

When a single loss of something you call "mine" can be so painful, imagine the moment of death when everything and everyone you call your own is suddenly taken away from you? When you see your own death approaching, all cords of attachment tied to various things you call "me" and "mine" will pull on your heart simultaneously. Will you still hold on to these attachments? Or will you choose to let go? If you remain adamant and identify yourself with the false

"I," and hold on to all the strings it ties itself to and calls "mine," the inevitable death of that entity brought about by snatching away all those things will cause a pain so deep that many have described the experience as going through "Hell." If letting go of one attachment is so difficult that it makes you lose sleep, will you be ready for the day when you have to let go of all of it? When death arrives, it often comes swiftly and unannounced. Are you prepared for it?

The simplest way to free yourself from suffering is to return to your true identity of Love. Just as letting go of a stick from your hand releases all the balloons tied to the stick, willingly letting go of the false identity "I," automatically releases all other attachments to the various forms it ties itself to as "mine." This ego entity "I" is going to suffer each time an object of its attachment gets pulled away from it. Instead of laboring to untie each and every knot of attachment from the stick, it's much simpler to let go of the stick altogether. In fact, mere renunciation of the various things you used to call "mine," without letting go of the ego which you call "I," will simply make the attachment to the ego even stronger. It is possible for a monk who's given up his possessions and lives in the mountains to have a much stronger ego than a person living in a palace with numerous possessions. With a stronger attachment to his ego, the monk may have an even tougher time letting go when the dream eventually approaches its end. It's not the shape of the dream; it's whether or not you're identified with the dreamer that determines if you're free or not. True renunciation is renunciation of the false "I" and returning to your true identity of love.

Loss is a wonderful opportunity to wake up from your false identity and return to love. Normally, when things are going very smoothly and the dream is very pleasant, no one wishes to wake up from it or even think about the inevitable end to the fleeting dream. People, in fact, take pride in their false ego and hold on even more strongly when things are pleasurable. But when you are trapped in a nightmare, and undergo tremendous loss, that's when you become desperate to wake up. In such desperation, it would be a mistake to try to end the dream forcefully by killing the dream body (suicide); for the whole world including the dream body is merely a projection of the dreamer you attach yourself to as "I." When you forcefully end the dream by killing the dream body, without dissolving attachment to the dream entity that you identify with, the "I" thought will create a new dream, a new projection that it can survive in. There's no guarantee that this new dream will be any better than your current nightmare. In all likelihood it will be much worse, a nightmare so bad, it will feel like Hell. Hell is not a permanent place you go to as suggested by certain religious scriptures; it's simply a nightmare created by complete forgetfulness of your true identity; an experience of separation from love so painful and lonely that even a short duration in that place can feel like eternity. It is the false identity "I" you need to wake up from; with it, all its projections will automatically disappear.

To wake up from that false identity, here's what you do:

When you find yourself worrying, arguing about, or losing sleep over the loss of the object you call "mine";

when you find yourself unable to let go of the attachment and powerless to stop the flood of compulsive thoughts that resist, complain and moan about your present condition; when the resulting restlessness and emotional turbulence make you cry in agony: it is in fact possible to just pause, smile and return to love. When you realize that by siding with these painful thoughts that refuse to let go, you are fighting a losing battle, don't take the opposite approach and criticize your inner state, saying: "I shouldn't be feeling this way and shouldn't harbor such thoughts." This will merely add to the noise and conflict in your head space. Instead, say: "I love the fact that such thoughts are happening. I love the fact that such feelings are arising. I love it that I am unable to let go. I love all of it." Open your heart and love it all. You will be amazed by the sudden transformation that follows.

Just as upon seeing his lost mother, the child abandons his toys and quickly returns to her lap, offering yourself unconditional love will snap you out of the head space and return you to the heart space. Siding with thoughts strengthens the "I" thought with attachment; opposing thoughts strengthens the "I" thought with guilt. When you neither side with thoughts nor criticize them, but love the fact that thoughts are happening, it helps you awaken from the dream identity of thinker into your true identity of love. The homing instinct of the heart instantly recognizes the presence of love, and will willingly let go of all attachments to the ego; it doesn't lose any time returning to the flow of love that offers true fulfillment.

The child who gets pleasure from playing with toys starts crying when those toys break or get taken away from him; but as soon as his mom arrives and showers her love upon him, he forgets the toys, gets wrapped up in her love and becomes cheerful again. Similarly, the moment you allow love into your awareness, your heart instantly remembers its true eternal nature and abandons any false association with the temporary entity, the "I" thought. At first you may feel some detachment, a separation from this entity that thinks and suffers; soon, just as a neighbor's pain doesn't touch you, the pain that once felt unbearable will now feel distant in the presence of love. As you continue to flow with love, you will feel a blissful release. The presence of true love suddenly awakens you from the nightmare of compulsive thinking and returns you to the sanctuary of love, your true abode. You find yourself returning to a familiar feeling of deep peace, lightness and joy. Once you awaken to reality, you will laugh out loud at how you took a dream life so seriously, often fighting, arguing, worrying and sweating over things that had no real existence apart from the dream. The things that used to bother you or irritate you trouble you no more.

When you encounter a loss and find yourself suffering in pain, unable to let go of thoughts of attachment, don't bother siding with the thoughts or opposing them. Simply bring yourself to love all of it. Drop all resistance. Love the loss, love the pain, love the fact that thoughts are happening, love that you're unable to let go. Returning to love awakens you from the nightmare of suffering and takes you back home to perfect stillness and abundant joy.

Similarly, when you find someone else in grief and see that they're unable to let go of the loss, offer them unconditional love. They'll come out of grief in their own time. There's no need to talk them out of suffering, as words are meaningless and ineffective when someone's trapped in pain. Just offer love. Just as a person who wants to save herself from drowning will spot a lifeline when it's offered to her, a heart that's desperate to wake up from a nightmare of thoughts will instantly grab on to love when offered. Please note, however, that the true meaning of offering love is to abide in your true identity of love. When thus established in love yourself, whatever you do from that space will be an offering of love. On the other hand, when you seek to help others while coming from a place of ego attachment, you will at best help them forget their suffering, not heal it. Egotistical help will merely help them move from one nightmare to another dream; it won't help them wake up.

Choose love now. It's time to wake up.

# Chapter XVII

## Fake Enlightenment vs. True Liberation: Part One

"Out of many thousands among men, one may endeavor for perfection, and of those who have achieved perfection, hardly one knows Me in truth." - Bhagavad Gita, Chapter 7, Verse 3

\*\*\*

A spiritual practitioner in the course of his or her practice will encounter various experiences and wonderful states. Developing attachments to such passing pleasant experiences will leave the practitioner in a state of suffering once those temporary states have passed. Mistaking these temporary states as ultimate Enlightenment would be a grave mistake. Such an attitude might lead one to slacken from practice, lose touch with the loving grace and revert to confusion and suffering. One such experience of a temporary state is illustrated below:

One fine Saturday afternoon, I was sitting in meditation. I kept releasing and letting go of all thoughts as they appeared and gradually sank myself into deep Self-absorption. After about 45 minutes or so had passed, a feeling of peace and joy came upon me, as it usually did during my meditations. The peace grew deeper and deeper and I felt a very pleasant sensation in the heart center in my chest. This pleasant sensation slowly spread to the rest of my body and enveloped my whole being. Even this wasn't too uncommon as I had experienced it on several occasions in the past during meditation. However, this feeling of deep peace and joy quickly flowered into a sense of abundant bliss that was so fulfilling that I let my whole being soak in it completely. It was as if a river of nectar was flowing through my veins. Even when I opened my bodily eyes, there was this deep undercurrent of peace, calm and joy within and without me. Although even this was not too uncommon after some good meditation sessions, this time I felt much more deeply rooted in the sense of peace and calm; no matter what anyone said or did, it didn't seem to shake me out of this center. Nothing that anyone did bothered or irritated me in the very least; things that used to trigger certain negative emotions didn't bother me anymore. A portion of my awareness was deeply drenched in this feeling of love that seemed to emanate from my spiritual heart center. The main awareness remained in blissful communion with the joy within. Almost no energy was being spent in judging or resisting anything or anyone. The feeling of love enveloped everything that appeared within and without. This state lasted several weeks, and no matter what I did, this feeling of joy and bliss did not leave me.

At times the peace and bliss would automatically draw me inward, and I would be led to drop all activities and get absorbed in the bliss of the Self. On some days, the state of bliss persisted throughout the day even without continuing formal meditation. Thoughts started appearing in my mind "Is this it? Is this what people call Enlightenment?" I even boasted to some of my friends about this "blissful state" as if to subtly suggest that I was superior in some way. I even started acting with some arrogance. I started getting overconfident, and slowly my spiritual practice began to slacken as I allowed the "superior" attitude to latch on to me. Since the activity of thought was quite minimal, I dropped my guard in the delusion that I had made a permanent entry into the heart space, the garden of eternal love. No one could ever knock me back into a state of compulsive thinking and suffering again, or so I thought. Since I had been feeling this for quite a while without any continued effort, this must be some kind of a permanent shift, right?

Wrong. When a small airplane runs out of fuel in mid-flight, it may continue to glide in midair for some time, but eventually it will come crashing down. It is stupidity to assume that the plane will continue to soar in the air without losing altitude. Such a plane is bound to crash sooner or later unless it lands to refuel. Similarly, when I started to get attached to this blissful state and slackened my spiritual practice and alertness, I had opened up the fuel tank and started losing altitude.

Meditation, as we have seen in previous chapters, is the art of returning to love, your true Self. Love neither resists anything that appears, nor does love try to grab onto something that is about to pass. Love just constantly flows releasing and loving everything on its way no matter what appears or disappears. When I tried to latch onto to this "Blissful state" that was passing by, I got stuck and disconnected myself from the flow of love. Slowly I watched love fade away from my awareness.

A month after the awakening experience, I was back in full ego-consciousness. Everything that used to bother me started bothering me again; every thought that used to irritate me, started irritating me again; and this time it was even worse than it used to be. When you take a poor person from the streets, and put him in a royal palace for some time, and then put him back on the streets - the contrast of the sudden reversal back into poverty from riches is pretty shocking. So when I fell from grace, the things that used to irritate me before, felt magnified in effect several fold.

The temporary state of bliss was just a vacation from my head space when my ego had temporarily weakened, allowing me a glimpse of what it would be like to live from the heart space, constantly releasing and loving every moment. I thought I could remain in that wonderful state forever, but as soon as I had tried to grab onto that state, I had already disconnected from the "heart that loves" and re-entered the "head that judges."

I could have connected back with love at any instant; simply loving everything "as is" in the moment would have immediately put me back into the stream of love. But I was too ignorant. I was too busy resisting the reversal to pain and suffering, and the more I resisted, the more it disconnected me from love and drove me deeper into the very suffering I was trying to avoid.

The following quote below aptly summarizes what happened:

"Further, in this state of *samadhi*, the good person sees the disintegration of the form *skandha* and understands the feeling *skandha*. In his refined understanding, he awakens completely to subtle principles. Everything is in accord with his wishes. He may suddenly experience limitless lightness and ease in his mind. He may say that he has become a sage and attained great self-mastery. This is called 'attaining lightness and clarity due to wisdom.' If he understands, then there is no error. This experience does not indicate sagehood.

"But if he considers himself a sage, then a demon that likes lightness and clarity will enter his mind. Claiming that he is already satisfied, he will not strive to make further progress. For the most part, such cultivators will become like the unlearned *Bhikshu*. He will mislead living beings so that they will fall into *Avichi* Hell. Lacking proper *samadhi*, he will certainly fall." - *Surangama Sutra: 50 Skanda Demon States* with commentary by Hsuang Hua

There are many practitioners who have similar spiritual or transcendental experiences for prolonged periods of time, and think that they are "Enlightened" or "Liberated." However, "Liberation" is not some kind of special experience or state that you can claim to possess so that you can show it off to your friends. ALL states are temporary; only YOU are permanent.

Any pleasure derived out of attachment to any state will result in suffering once the state passes. Flowing with love, your true nature, regardless of whatever state comes into your awareness is what brings true fulfillment.

With this dawns the understanding: Liberation is not FOR the ego; Liberation is FROM the ego.

Liberation is from the ego that judges.

Liberation is from the ego that resists the "unpleasant."

Liberation is from the ego that grabs on to the "pleasant."

Liberation is to return to the love that flows.

# Chapter XVIII

## Fake Enlightenment Vs. True Liberation: Part Two

"If asked: 'Which of these three is final liberation: - with form, without form, or with and without form?' I say, 'Liberation is the extinction of the ego which inquires 'With form, without form, or with and without form?" - *"Reality in 40 Verses"* by Sri Ramana Maharshi

\*\*\*

The ego is a separate sense of self derived by separating oneself from the rest of existence, and by identifying with a temporary body with a bunch of thoughts and experiences. Water evaporates from the surface of the ocean, becomes part of a cloud and precipitates again onto earth as rain fall. Similarly, the ego is like a tiny rain drop that has separated itself from the mighty ocean of infinite consciousness. Some drops gather to become a pond, some become a lake, some become a puddle, but no matter how big the drops become, they will still be minuscule compared to the rest of the mighty ocean, their true source. Hence, no matter how big one's achievements, one will still find oneself lacking and incomplete as long as one considers oneself to be separate from the rest of totality. Until the drop returns to the ocean, it will continue to feel that it has much more to achieve, and will know no lasting peace.

Similarly, until a soul reunites with infinite consciousness, it will continue to feel inadequacy and suffering. If a spiritual practitioner takes pride in his achievements and spiritual experiences, this will strengthen his ego which will seek to fill the inherent void (due to identification with a limited ego) by seeking the adoration and worship of followers. All spiritual progress (toward liberation) for the practitioner comes to a full stop, and he becomes trapped in an ego that leads to his eventual downfall and reversal to a state of suffering.

An incident experienced by the author is worth mentioning in relation to this topic: Once I was meditating outside the house of a sage (I don't mention the name of the sage, as she prefers to lead a very reclusive life). The sage was walking around the house as was part of her daily evening routine. I had been meditating outside her house several hours a day for the past couple of days, waiting for a private audience with her. I had just arrived from a different country to stay with and learn from the sage. I had met the sage once a few years ago, and my heart was totally captivated by her grace. I had since been corresponding with her and had been trying to practice her teachings.

The sage was known to put disciples to various kinds of tests before granting them a private audience. After the first two days meditating outside the house, the initial peace and tranquility that I felt slowly faded away as I was growing somewhat impatient. It started to bother me that someone who was as qualified and sincere as myself (or so I imagined in my egotistical arrogance) was being denied a private audience. When the sage walked by me, I smiled and waved at her hoping to catch her attention; she looked at me and did not even acknowledge my presence or return my smile. She turned away and kept walking. I grew more irritated and impatient and my meditation became disturbed with various kinds of thoughts and emotions, and I was getting filled with doubts, judgments and even anger. I saw some people being summoned for private audience with the sage, and I started becoming envious and judgmental and even started doubting if this was a real sage or not. My mind argued that otherwise she would have surely recognized that I deserved a private audience more than these people who seemed to be (according to my mind) more "materialistic" and less "spiritual" than myself. These thoughts were baseless, as I had had the opportunity to witness and experience amazing grace pouring out of this sage on several occasions over the past two years of my association with her (through phone); and in return she had never accepted anything from me: no gifts, no money, nor praise. Yet caught up in the ego, I was having all these doubts and suspicions.

After the third day, I realized what I was doing. I had identified myself with my ego. My ego wanted to have this private audience with the sage so that it could feel good about itself and say, "Look, I am special. That's why I get to meet the sage privately and get her love and attention, while many others do not." When the ego was being denied its desire, it was causing irritation, anger and suspicion. I laughed out loud at this realization and let all the desires and doubts go. I no longer desired any private audience with the sage; I no longer wanted her to smile back at me or acknowledge my presence; I no longer wanted to feel special or loved. I no longer even wished for the lingering emotions to go away. I no longer wanted anything from anyone, and just was content the way I was in the fullness of the moment. I just let all thoughts and desires go; and slowly the heavy emotions dissipated, and peace and calm dawned upon me.

"When you demand nothing of the world, nor of God, when you want nothing, seek nothing, expect nothing, then the Supreme state will come to you uninvited and unexpected." - Nisargadatta Maharaj

I was meditating outside the sage's house when she left for an evening walk. As she walked by, I happened to open my eyes and they met the sage's loving gaze. I closed my eyes again as she walked past me and a deep sense of joy and love enveloped me from within and tears started trickling down my eyes. The intensity of joy overflowed within me and it felt as if I was being slowly drawn into a mighty ocean of love. Every particle of my being was filled with the nectar that was pouring out of this ocean. There are no words to express that experience; the closest words are "infinite love bliss." I felt as if I was drenched in an ocean of endless bliss. I don't know how long I had been there, when I started losing awareness of my body and began to merge with this being of love. It was as if I was losing my identity and merging with this infinite being of love, call it God, call it the Supreme Self or what you may.

The whole world as I knew it was disappearing and the only feeling I was aware of was of this infinite love and bliss. I did not wish to come out of it. Suddenly, a fearful thought appeared in my mind: "Wait, is this it?

Is this the end? It would be really boring if I just kept feeling endless joy and nothing else. It would be boring not to have other people or other experiences around." I was shocked that my ego was still alive and even more shocking that I was latching onto it instead of surrendering myself to this ocean of love that was opening itself to me. I wasn't yet ready to give up identity as a separate self. I wasn't ready to give up the world of pleasure and pain. Here was God-Self, the supreme spirit, opening his door and inviting me in, offering me infinite timeless joy and love; and here I was hesitating to enter. I was unable to bring myself to let go of my separate sense of identity and surrender myself into the arms of this wonderful impersonal being. I realized that I wasn't ready to give up my ego identity. Perhaps, I thought, I need to suffer a lot more before I am ready for this surrender. My wish was about to come true, but I had no idea that it would be so soon.

In the days to follow, during meditations, instead of letting go of my thoughts, I started identifying with them and feeding them with my attention. And slowly but surely the feeling of abundant joy whose floodgates had temporarily opened a few days back, started to fade away from my awareness. I found myself back in ego-consciousness. I was back in a miserable state of lack, neediness and fear. I tried every meditation "technique" I knew, but nothing worked. I wrote a note to the sage asking to teach me so that I could let go of my ego and return to the bliss of the Self. My message did not evoke any response. I found myself getting more drawn into the ego-identified state and grew irritated and angry again. I started having angry thoughts about the sage and her teaching methods. Instead of owning my mistakes, I started blaming her for my present condition of misery. "When she meets me I am going to give her a piece of my mind," I thought, "and tell her how ineffective her teachings are. Why is she making me sit outside for so long? Why isn't she responding to my messages and questions?"

I felt someone tapping on my shoulder and pointing me to enter the gate of the Sage's house. "Busted!" I thought.

The person came with a message from the sage. He told me, "The sage is receiving negative vibrations from you, so she has no choice but to send you away. She won't be able to give you a private audience as she doesn't sense any heart connection from you. She feels that you aren't ready for this and hence should leave." I was heartbroken! I was already in a miserable state totally disconnected from love. The only one I knew then who could get me out of this miserable state, the one I had relied upon over the last two years to lift me back into the abode of love, had suddenly withdrawn from my life. My only lifeline was gone. Foolishly, I had shot myself in the foot. I was shattered.

Over the next few days I experienced a pain so deep that it can only be compared to mourning the loss of a dear one. I couldn't shake myself out of this grief. I felt incredible pain in my being, as if my heart had been ripped apart from my soul.

The sage, as a part of her message, had told me that I could stay for a few more days and meditate outside her house should I so desire. However, after two days was up, I was to leave quietly and should never contact her again. I took her up on her offer and meditated outside her house. Meditation was probably not the right word to describe what I was doing, for meditation is to let go of identification with your thoughts and remain in awareness of your true Self. On the contrary, I was in complete identification with my miserable thoughts; and the emotional pain I experienced as a result was unbearable. I felt like I was being stabbed with a million knives from within.

Just two days ago, I was floating in cloud nine at the gates of heaven with an invitation to swim in timeless joy. But I hesitated and thought, "Wait, this is too soon. Endless joy seems quite boring. I need to experience more suffering before I am ready for this." Fast forward two days ahead and I found myself in the worst of hells. Never before in this lifetime had I experienced so much pain. The thought of suicide did briefly cross my mind, but I ruled it out as I didn't want to pass on the pain to my parents who loved me dearly. Intuitively I knew that suicide doesn't end the pain, it only increases the karmic burden. It's better to endure what is given here and now, rather than to postpone it for later.

I sat there in front of the sage's house trying my best to meditate and let go of these crazy thoughts creating such intolerable pain inside of me. The pain was so intense that sitting there was agonizing. I had completely forgotten the simple truth that all I had to do was to bring self-love instead of self-judgment or self-righteousness to my feelings and that would help me return from a state of suffering to love. Instead I was caught in this whirlpool of judgmental thoughts that were leading me in a downward spiral sucking my soul further and further away from love. I just wanted to run away. But where would I run? Wherever I went, there I was; so there would be no point in running anywhere. So I just kept sitting there, waiting for the storm to pass.

The sage was going on her evening walk and our eyes met. I looked at her to see if there was any sympathy in her eyes? The answer came almost instantly, I noticed her eyes were wet; tears were streaming down her cheeks as she kept her loving gaze directed at me while she walked past. It was as if she was telling me telepathically: "Oh dear one, what have you done? Why did you forsake me even when I had my arms wide open? I had no other recourse but to send you away for I have to honor your choice." Any residual anger or doubts that might still be lingering in my mind completely disappeared. I realized that it was completely my fault. I was indeed not ready. I had to go through all this pain and drama to realize how precious and sacred the state I had turned away from was. I wasn't ready to let go of my ego and merge into this ocean of abundant love, my true Self.

All these years that I had been on the spiritual journey, I used to think that I was ready for liberation, and really wanted it. However, I realized that I was far from ready. I would have to go through many more life experiences before I would be ready for complete surrender to supreme love, our true source.

It is extremely rare to encounter someone who desires true and complete liberation from the Ego. Almost no one wants it. We love the drama; we love the suffering; often we like to take a break or a vacation from the ego-identified state for it can be quite draining and tiresome; however, any talk about ending the ego, and the ego will run the opposite way.

Even at the time of physical death, there is an opening when a soul may be given a choice to merge back into this state of oneness with infinite love-bliss-awareness. Yet few souls are ready to choose final liberation. Most, still in the ego-identified state, will choose to retain their ego and return to the cycle of birth and death. And since the ego is responsible for all suffering, until it ends there can be no true liberation. But since the ego rarely ever wants to end, it is a vicious cycle of a thief trying to play the cop. This self-deception leads people to believe that they want spiritual liberation while they don't really want liberation. This may lead them to seek temporary experiences which can give them an illusion of being enlightened while still being trapped in an ego-identified state. However, a truly honest person will realize the absurdity of the possibility of liberation (state of oneness) existing side by side with an active ego that separates itself from "others" and claims to be "holier than thou."

Self-honesty helps a lot. With self-honesty, we will know that experiencing temporary states of bliss doesn't make us more enlightened than others. As long as the ego, the separate sense of identity exists, the journey is incomplete.

We may not be ready for complete self-surrender just yet, but we can continue to get glimpses of the "ego-free" state through meditation by letting go of the thoughts in our head, and returning to the love in our heart. As we keep spending more time with our true Self (abiding as love in the heart) and less time with the ego (thoughts in our head), our love for our Self will keep growing and our attachment to the ego will keep decreasing. Our heart will recognize that Love is indeed our true home and it's not worth leaving it even for a moment.

As you keep flowing with the river of love, a day will arrive when this river will discharge back into the mighty ocean of infinite consciousness. The drop returns home and becomes one with its source. Upon becoming one with the ocean, then there are no "other" drops, there is just one mighty ocean. Your heart just melts in the supreme joy of this reunion. Everywhere you look, there is only supreme love and endless bliss.

Flow with the river of love and come back home. The ocean of Love awaits your return.

# Chapter XIX

## Love is Independent of Action or Inaction

Love is not an action.

Action can be done with or without love.

Action with love flows naturally and effortlessly, as a joyful expression of love.

Action without love feels burdensome, and requires exertion to overcome the mental resistance and inner conflict.

Love is not inaction either.

Mere inaction is to hold on to a particular physical or mental position.

To hold on to something in conflict with your inner desire, or despite the inevitable circumstantial changes, requires effort.

Love doesn't hold; it just flows with "what is," effortlessly.

When you return to the flow of love, you may appear to be in dynamic action to all external appearances; but internally you are in a state of effortlessness and peaceful harmony.

On the other hand, someone might appear to be sitting still, holding on to a rigid physical posture, but internally might be in a state of intense mental activity and resistance.

To love means to be in a state of effortlessness and harmony in relation to the present moment; whether the moment takes the shape of physical rest or activity is immaterial.

## Break Free from the Spell of "Urgent" Thoughts

Thoughts that demand urgent attention are rarely as urgent as they pretend to be. If faced with a life-threatening situation or to avoid a potentially disruptive situation (e.g.: if you're about to miss a flight), by all means hurry up and attend to it immediately. Aside from those exceptions, however, whenever you sense urgency from within, pause and ask yourself: "How am I feeling now?"

Do you sense serenity, joy and lightness? Those are your true companions when you abide in the heart space of love. When you rush along and heed the urgency of thoughts, you are more likely to find yourself in foreign territory surrounded by restlessness, anxiety and emotional turbulence. Acting or speaking under the spell of such restless emotions is similar to driving under the influence of an intoxicant. It will lead to a bumpy ride if not to a fatal accident. If the quality or outcome of this "urgent" activity or conversation is important to you, slow down a little. Acting or speaking impulsively upon invitation of these "urgent" thoughts may land you in hot water. Before you rush to the decision, or to make the phone call, pause, breathe and Return to love. It may save you from a disaster.

Meditation is your best friend to help you slow down and Return you to love (See Chapter X: Meditation and the Art of Returning to Love and Chapter XXIII: Guided Meditation: Being a Loving Presence). But how do you convince yourself to meditate when you're under the spell of thoughts that urge you to immediate action? If you task yourself to sit for an hour-long meditation, your mind will likely rebel at the idea and may become even noisier. Instead, bait yourself by saying: "I am just going to sit on the meditation cushion for one minute. I am not going to meditate for too long, but maybe just one minute." Most activities aren't so urgent that they cannot even wait one minute. Your mind's likely to be a lot more receptive to the idea of breaking for "just one minute" than for a longer time. So go ahead, and with the consent of your mind take a break from the activity and sit down with yourself for a minute. Let go of the urgent thoughts for a short moment and wrap yourself with unconditional love. After you sit for a minute, and feel a little bit of peace, bait yourself again: "Ah! This feels good; maybe I will sit for few more minutes." Sensing some peace, the homing instincts of your heart will be triggered which relaxes its attachment to the ego and looks forward to return to home. Thoughts no longer have the same power over you and you find that the task that couldn't wait at all can suddenly wait a few more minutes. As you sit for five more minutes releasing thoughts and returning to love, you will get hooked in, and start enjoying it. Once you sense yourself returning to the coolness of love and the stillness of being, you'll suddenly recall that your inner state is completely independent of external situations. What felt so "urgent" and "important" just a little while ago may not feel as important as returning to the purity of your true being. Keep sitting for however long it takes to return to the purity of love and enjoy returning home to your true companions of peace, joy and stillness. Your perspective broadens and clarity returns. Untainted by the restlessness that often accompanies attachment to how things should or should not be, your action will flow gracefully in perfect harmony with "what is," a joyful creation born out of loving communion with passion and clarity. Or you may realize that no action is required at all, and the original urge was simply a craving toward a meaningless activity, an ego distraction far removed from your heart's true desire.

Break free from the spell of urgent thoughts, and give yourself the gift of love. Your actions will be graceful and your efforts meaningful.

# Chapter XX

## Nine Keys to Harmony in Relationship

"Relationship is a mirror." – J. Krishnamurti

\*\*\*

Relationships serve as a mirror to reflect your inner state. Disharmonious relationships are a sign that you are trapped in your headspace, in thoughts of judgment. Harmonious interpersonal relationships are the result of abiding in the heart space as love.

There are nine keys to help stay in the heart space as love and promote harmony in relationships.

They are:

- Key # 1: Principle of Abundance
- Key # 2: Sincere Humility and Gratitude
- Key # 3: Non-criticism
- Key # 4: Be Free of Suspicion
- Key # 5: Attentive Presence

- Key # 6: True Generosity
- Key # 7: *Brahmacharya*
- Key # 8: Prayer for Love, Healing and Harmony
- Key # 9: Learn to Laugh

Please note that these keys are not something that you have to "do" in order to become a "good" person. Both "good" and "bad" are value judgments that happen in the head space; they have little meaning in the heart space. "Bad" people abuse others and make others miserable; "good" people tolerate abuse and often make *themselves* miserable! "I am a bad person" and "I am a good person" are both ego identities created by identifying with mental projections. Don't get me wrong; goodness is indeed a virtue, but only when it flows naturally from your heart established in your true identity of Love. When you feel like doing something that others might perceive as "bad," but you suppress it and force yourself to do "good" just to win approval or because some book or philosopher told you it's the "right" thing to do, it will merely make you sorrowful. You may fool a few people around you with the fake smile on your face, but you won't be able to fool your heart when it sheds tears of sorrow. You will then wonder, "Why am I feeling so bad even when I do so much 'good' to others?" When your heart is not in harmony with your actions, it doesn't matter what or how much you do, it will create further disharmony within and without. Initially people may praise you for all the "good" you do, but as your frustration builds up from within, eventually it will spill over into your words and actions. People will sense this inner frustration; that's what they will pick up on, not your external actions no matter how "good" they are. Some people try to earn admission into heaven for their "good" actions while they subject themselves to suffering in an internal hell. There's no need to torture yourself like that. You can experience heaven here and now, not by doing things the world considers "good," but simply by returning to love in your heart. Whether people perceive you to be "good" or "bad," love yourself unconditionally. Whether some person or situation you encounter is considered "good" or "bad," love them anyway. Even if you sense "bad" feelings arise toward someone or something, just love it. It's never too late to love. Whatever may be your inner or outer state, don't criticize it, just love it. When you shut the door of your heart to feelings, situations or people by calling them "bad," they may bang on the door even louder creating an inner turmoil that torments you, demanding your attention. Instead, keep the door of your heart open; welcome everyone and everything with love. Any feelings of judgment will quickly pass and leave through the same door, returning you to the experience of peace and natural bliss of being.

This bliss you perceive out of inner harmony will eventually radiate to those around you. The moment you choose love, it puts you in touch with the true goodness that naturally flows from your heart. When you invite love inside your heart, it's doesn't matter what you do after that; it will radiate true goodness and create true peace and harmony.

The keys presented below are not an ideal that you need to strive toward; they are simply reminders of the goodness that's already inherent in you. Constant remembrance of the goodness and harmony within makes us more alert should we ever slip from it into a non-loving and disharmonious state. Whenever your slip into such disharmonious states, *prajna,* the light of awareness within will warn you. Simply heed the warning, apply the brakes of *pratikraman,* and return to love. It is worth remembering that in order to return to the purity of love, your natural state, you have to spend enough time in daily meditation or prayer. Just as you need to shower every day to cleanse the impurities from your body, you need to meditate or pray every day, often multiple times a day, to shake off the thoughts that make you forget your true identity of love. Every time you feel disconnected from love, go meditate or pray and let the nectar of grace bathe you in love. Without daily spiritual practice, love simply remains as a concept in your head and you may find it really challenging to apply the principles that put love into action. Love, the experience, soothes and heals; love as an intellectual concept merely adds to the noise in the head. Through daily spiritual practice, it will become much easier to return to and abide in the experience of true love and harmony.

Let the following keys serve to unlock the goodness in you whenever you find yourself lost or shut out in disharmony.

## Key #1: Principle of Abundance

Spirit, your true essence, is needless and self-content. The body, on the other hand, has many needs. When you stay aware of your true identity, you experience abundant love and fulfillment. Hence the "principle of abundance" is to stay focused on the source of true abundance, the spirit within. When you are thus focused on inner fulfillment, the needs of the body are few and there is "plenty to go around." When you stay rooted in this realization that there is plenty to go around, you feel constant love from within and never feel threatened by anything or anyone. You will experience constant inner peace and outer harmony.

Instead, when you shift from alignment with spirit into identification with the limited mortal body, it draws you away from love and abundance and centers you in fear and inadequacy. Scientists have associated the limbic part of the brain with the survival instinct of animals. When we operate from this region of the brain, we become fearful and go into "survival of the fittest" mentality. While we operate from this mode, we forget our abundance and become envious of others, develop feelings of ill will and jealousy, we criticize and complain, seek attention, and so on. Even very educated and professional people can potentially become rapists and murderers when this part of the brain is stimulated. Even spiritually "advanced" gurus sometimes fall into lust and greed and get involved in unimaginable scandals when they forget the essence of spirit and come under the influence of the primitive part of the brain that favors "survival of the fittest." Constant remembrance of the "principle of abundance"' is the best way to counter the illusion of lack. Whenever you see someone succeed, be happy for them; join in the celebration and cherish the good feelings. There is plenty to go around. There is no need to fear that there might not be enough for your happiness. Your happiness doesn't depend on anything in the outside world. Abundant joy and immeasurable love is closer than breathing. It is available for you in abundance. No one is your competitor. When you find the wealth within, you become an example for others to discover within themselves. You become everyone's friend. Remember this and fear not your neighbor, nor envy their worldly success. Just remain aware of your inner abundance and spread love and goodwill, and good things will follow even in the outer world.

## Key# 2: Sincere Humility and Gratitude

"There are no independent doers in this universe." – Dadashri

As spirit, you are self-content and truly independent of anything outside of you. But in the world of relative existence, no man is an island. For anything you need to accomplish in this physical world, you need the help of others. Only the biggest of egotists can claim, "I did this all by myself." And there would be no truth in that statement. Even in a simple activity like writing and publishing this book, the help of so many tools and people are needed: a computer, word processing software, people to help with editing, proofreading, cover design, printing, etc. This book couldn't be written and published in its current shape without: the people who contributed to the invention and manufacture of the tools highlighted above, the individual contributors in each step of publication, schools that shaped the minds and talents of these people, the sages and role models that inspired the author, not to mention the evolution of the English language itself. Even after the books are printed and distributed, true success in publication rests in the hands of readers like you who purchase and read the book and recommend it to their friends. As Isaac Newton once said, "We stand on the shoulders of giants." Everything in this world is inter-related. Each and every particle in the universe has some influence and effect on every other particle. Even tiny organisms like earth-worms play an important role in replenishing the nutrients in the soil and help grow the vegetation that feeds humanity and other animal species. Once the realization dawns that no accomplishment made in the relative world is truly independent, it automatically makes you humble. The presence of humility brings to your awareness the numerous people who have contributed to your life in meaningful ways directly or indirectly, and makes your heart overflow with gratitude and appreciation. When you give sincere appreciation to the people in your everyday world, it brings awareness to the goodness in your life. Instead, when you lack humility and get stuck in egotistical thoughts such as: "Look how much I do; yet I don't get appreciated enough," it shifts your awareness from a feeling of abundance to one of inadequacy and loneliness. It may trigger emotions like pride and jealousy, creating divisions between you and other people and resulting in disharmonious interactions. Often, we focus on what's missing in our lives and forget about what's present. It should be the other way around.

Reflect on the people who play a role in your everyday life. Start with your family members and your close friends, all the way to the people who contribute to your life in simple ways: the cashier at the grocery store, the mailman, the garbage collector, the janitor at the office, the customer service rep on the phone, etc. Look for opportunities to express gratitude toward them. Show sincere appreciation to your mom or spouse when they cook you a special meal, the cashier or waiter who is considerate and kind, the customer service rep on the phone who was helpful, the people who take the time to call you or write to you. You don't have to do express it verbally, although you are most welcome to; but remember, verbal appreciation with no feeling in the heart is meaningless. It's enough if you express with your heart: through a smile, through sweetness in the tone of your voice, a hug, a positive thought, a prayer, a friendly laugh, a kiss or with attentive presence. When true humility is present in your heart and you feel gratitude toward the person in front of you, they will sense it even if no words are spoken. It will do wonders for your relationship.

## Key #3: Non-criticism

If we are like most people, not only do we not appreciate the ones around us for the things they do for us, but we also often complain and criticize when they fail to meet our expectations. When you criticize the negatives and fail to appreciate the positives, it is a recipe for deterioration in a relationship. If there's something important to you that you feel is not being addressed adequately, use loving communication to express your views. You can also be assertive, but it should always be accompanied by calmness and never with aggressiveness. To be assertive is to stand up for your rights; to be aggressive is to do so at the cost of violating someone else's rights. That's a fine line that you shouldn't cross, lest you cause disharmony in your relationships and lose inner peace. If you find yourself losing your cool, go for a walk or do something else to regain your equanimity. Just as arrows discharged from a bow cannot be retracted, the words that come out of your mouth cannot be taken back. Critical words can lodge into the memory of the listener and repeat themselves as painful thoughts, causing them torment and doing irreparable damage to your relationship. Hence, observe due caution with speech; seek to remain non-critical, and find ways to resolve tense situations with grace and aplomb. You may even write an email (or letter) to the person and pen down all the angry thoughts you have about them to let off some steam, but promptly delete the email (or shred the letter) after you cool down.

(Make sure you don't put anyone's address in the "To" field to avoid accidentally sending it out!)

If someone is overwhelmed with emotions and talks to you about irrelevant things in an irreverent way, do not engage them in an argument or it will make them even more emotional and defensive. Just stay calm, and listen patiently if you can. If they become aggressive, consider removing yourself from the emotionally charged situation; go for a walk or do anything else to give them the space to calm down. Just like a person drunk on alcohol, a person drunk with emotions is incapable of understanding logic. If you try to argue with them or prove them wrong, you too will get charged with emotions and it will make the situation even worse. The best course is to avoid getting emotionally involved. When you stay calm, you allow them the space to return to calmness. Remember, their true nature, like yours, is that of love, though their current state may not be reflective of this. When you see the reflection of the moon on the surface of a disturbed pond, it may give an appearance of a broken moon. If you keep stirring the surface, the disturbance will never cease. However, when you allow the water surface to return to stillness, it will perfectly reflect the image of the beautiful moon in its full glory. Similarly, when people are stirred up with emotions, it hides their true inner beauty. When you allow people to feel and express painful emotions without trying to change or correct them with criticism, they will naturally come back to their natural state of love once the emotions settle. Instead, if you criticize and argue with them, it will prolong the emotional disturbance and worse, they may hold you responsible for it and maintain a grudge and the caustic atmosphere will be prolonged. When you allow them to be upset while yourself staying calm, you give them the opportunity and space for self-reflection and aid a natural return to stillness; with this realization they find their way back to their inner calm and will be grateful to you for being supportive and understanding when they felt troubled.

## Key# 4: Be Free of Suspicion

Whether or not others are being honest, or if they will finish the task given to them in a timely or successful manner, is their responsibility, not yours. Your responsibility is toward your own actions, speech and intentions; even in your own case, you'll notice that circumstances may steer you off course and force you to make mistakes despite your best laid plans. The same is true with others. Mistakes, delays and differences of opinion may happen, but as soon as you start to suspect someone's motives and harbor negative thoughts about their intents, you spoil your own inner intents. Harboring suspicion causes anxiety, worry and fear and takes you far away from your natural state of love. Love doesn't suspect anyone; love places trust in "what is" and in its own ability to flow around it. Suspicion is an act of the judgmental head and it disconnects you from love. When you trust others by seeing the purity their heart is capable of expressing, you serve as a mirror reflecting to them their highest potential. When your own intentions are pure, no one else can deceive you.

Even if someone takes advantage of your goodness, it will only increase your own joy, not decrease it. When you give happiness to others, whether it's through voluntary generosity or through some involuntary means, it will get reflected back to you all the same. The only time you can truly get deceived is when you forget the wealth within and act out of some external expectation of gain. When your actions are motivated by such external expectations and you feel no joy in your heart while doing them, you will feel deceived when those expectations are not met. But if you retain awareness of your inner abundance and are honest to yourself, and act not out of expectation but as an expression of the love within, you will feel no regret or resentment even if the motives of the other person are indeed perverted. You will instead feel sympathy for them and be able to forgive them and move on.

Others may sometimes act out of ignorance of their true nature, and seek to deceive you. But they won't be deceiving anyone but themselves. They may successfully grab hold of a little of your external wealth or trick you to do some work for them, but in the process they will develop greed and deceit which makes them forget their inner abundance, and will sooner or later find themselves in suffering. They cannot steal your true wealth, the sanctuary of love within. When you spoil your own inner intent, you voluntarily lose touch with this inner abundance and lose yourself in anxiety, grief and resentment. So don't worry about what the intentions of others are; just keep your own intentions pure, and stay vigilant not to leave the inner sanctuary of love.

Seek to be free of suspicion within. You may take all the necessary precautions needed in the external world, but internally, put your trust in the goodness of others and in your own ability to love. When things don't go your way, give others the benefit of doubt instead of harboring suspicion. This will help preserve inner equanimity and harmony; by being centered in internal peace, any communication you have is bound to bring about external harmony.

## Key#5: Attentive Presence

Have you ever seen someone who's physically present but mentally absent? Have you ever tried to say something to someone but they were completely spaced out? They may have been lost in their own thoughts or preoccupied with their smart phone, computer or TV show; blissfully unaware of what you were saying, they may have even shooed you off to return to their la la land. Have you been at the receiving end of such inattentiveness? How did it feel? This is exactly how other people feel when you space out and disconnect yourself from the present moment, when you get lost in thoughts or preoccupy yourself with something that's not as real as the person in front of you.

The best gift you can give to those around you is your attentive, loving presence. And one of the best ways to do that is by grounding your attention in your body. Your body is connected to the present moment through the five senses, and by grounding your attention in the body, you can awaken from the dream of thinking into the awareness of being. As someone speaks to you, stay grounded and listen. This will help you from getting lost in the thoughts in your head and permit you to return to the love in your heart and be present to the person in front of you. I have found the

Alexander technique described in a later section (see Chapter XXV: Recommended Reading and Resources) to be very useful in this regard. I highly recommend it to others who wish to cultivate present moment awareness.

## Key#6: True Generosity

When you give happiness to others, it gets reflected back to you. When someone comes knocking on your door asking for help, strive to be generous with them. These opportunities may present themselves in small ways: it may be your spouse asking for your help with cooking or cleaning or a co-worker asking for assistance with a project; it may be a homeless person approaching you for a dollar, your child seeking your guidance with her assignment, an employee or contractor asking for a raise, etc. You don't have to travel to some far-off country to help a starving child (although you're most welcome to if you so desire); it is enough if you are generous with the people who show up in your day-to-day life. Charity begins at home. There are some people who claim they want to help the whole world, but they may be mean to their own family members and to the people around them. It is much more meaningful and impactful to make a true and deep connection with a few people around you than to make a superficial connection with millions of people in the world. Seek to be generous, not in a showy, theatrical fashion, but in simple and subtle ways toward people you connect with in your everyday life.

True generosity is that which flows naturally from your heart. When you express true generosity, you will feel the joy flowering in your heart. If this joy is absent, and you make a show of generosity to show off or just to do the "right" thing, make no mistake, it's not generosity at all. When you donate a dollar with a joyful heart, it's much better than donating ten with anticipation of approval or praise. The former is true generosity, while the latter is business. Be just as generous as you can afford to be. You don't have to give so much that it makes your own life difficult; as long as whatever you give brings joy to your heart, it is the right amount of generosity. Sometimes when asked for a favor and saying "Yes" doesn't feel right or convenient to your heart, it's all right to say "No." A "No" to someone else is still a "Yes" to your own heart! There's nothing wrong in being generous with yourself. As you keep being generous within the limits your heart feels comfortable with, you will notice that your heart's willingness as well as your physical ability and circumstances to give keep on growing. Generosity allows you to discover your inner strength. It brings into your awareness the inherent wealth inside of you that increases with sharing. You will experience a deep fulfillment that rarely, if ever, comes from amassing huge fortunes for yourself. Be generous with your smiles, your laughs, your words, the tone of your voice, your intentions, and maybe even your money, but only to the extent your heart says "Yes." It will enrich your life in many ways.

## Key# 7: *Brahmacharya* (Celibacy in mind, speech and body):

When you depend on external circumstances being a certain way for you to be happy, you will have innumerable expectations of others; your inner state will be at the mercy of those expectations always being met and it will take you on a roller-coaster ride of emotions. Such dependency will make you feel lonely and anxious. As we saw earlier, your true essence is that of boundless, deathless spirit. When you stay centered in your true identity of spirit, you experience true contentment and bliss, the wealth within that's independent of the external world. The way to experience the wealth within is *Brahmacharya*. *Brahman* means absolute consciousness or spirit (not to be confused with the word *Brahma*, the deity that represents creation) and *acharya* means lifestyle or practice. By sincerely experimenting with a lifestyle centered on the spirit instead of a lifestyle focused on pampering the body, you will discover that your life is fulfilling and free beyond imagination. Not only does such a lifestyle nourish you, but it will nourish anyone who comes in contact with you.

By no means is *Brahmacharya* an easy practice. It takes commitment, dedication and wisdom to practice it sincerely with mind, speech and body. But after the initial few months of challenges, the rewards that follow are many. It can do wonders for your health, spiritual progress and most importantly, relationships. You will feel constant joy and experience radiant health and unconditional love. You will start relating with others through your heart chakra (the heart chakra is symbolic of love) instead of relating through the root or sacral chakra (the root chakra and sacral chakra are symbolic of survival and reproduction instincts, respectively). You will discover the meaning of true unconditional love, and not only you but everyone who comes in touch with you will be blessed by the connection with the spirit in which you are grounded.

Please note that *Brahmacharya* is a holistic practice; it is not limited to physical celibacy but requires total involvement of your whole mind, speech and body. If you are physically practicing celibacy while you are actively thinking about sex in your mind, it will lead to suppression and inner conflict. Before you commence *Brahmacharya* practice, sit alone with yourself and talk to your body, your senses and your mind and ask them: "Hey body, will you cooperate with me; eyes, will you cooperate with me; ears, will you cooperate with me in this practice of celibacy?" etc. Each sense organ as well as your mind has to co-operate with you. 100% sincerity is required. Otherwise, one single lustful look or thought can throw you off. Gently sit with yourself, take your time and make a decision, "I am going to sincerely adopt a *Brahmacharya* lifestyle for X months." (I'd advise at least nine months to observe the full benefits). It is important that you remain strong during the initial challenging months when the body and mind experience withdrawal and detox symptoms. If you give up prematurely, you will never discover the bliss of self-contentment. You have to meditate every day, retaining connection with your inner abundance for successful observance of a *Brahmacharya* practice. In the Bhagavad Gita, Lord Krishna states: "Of various penances, I am *Brahmacharya*." It has been extolled as the best of disciplines in various scriptures of all religions and is indeed a worthy endeavor that will enrich you in various ways. It can also help heal the karmic baggage and emotional pain from past relationships and help you start fresh.

Do consider experimenting with a *Brahmacharya* lifestyle and learn about its benefits firsthand. You will find more elaboration on the topic of *Brahmacharya* in "Chapter XXI: Rise above the Illusion of Pleasure."

## Key #8: Prayer for Love, Healing and Harmony

You may be familiar with the concept of "Paying it forward." When you do a good deed for someone, it promotes the tendency in them to be good to the next person they meet. You will observe that not only do people pay it forward with good deeds and good feelings, but they do so with hurtful feelings as well. When someone is behaving in a seemingly hurtful way toward you, it is very possible that it has little or nothing to do with you at all. Don't take it personally. Maybe they had a bad day, got yelled at by their boss, got cut off in traffic, are overburdened with work, etc., and are taking the stress out on you. Avoid engaging them in an argument unless you'd like to get infected with the disharmonious virus yourself. Instead, return to love and pray sincerely that the concerned person experiences healing from the hurtful emotions that are causing them to behave in a way that's alien to their true nature.

Below is a sample procedure for the prayer:

Go to a secluded place if possible (when it gets easier for you to return to love, you can even do this effectively in non-secluded places). First, pray for love for yourself (or meditate) so that you can return to your true nature of love and let the feeling of love flood every cell of your being, cleansing you of any judgments or negative opinions. (See Chapter XI: Prayer for Love)

Harboring negative opinions about others is self-defeating in two ways: first, it creates misunderstanding; secondly, projecting negative thoughts has a further negative influence on the behavior of the person about whom you have such thoughts. A person's current behavior is a result of several factors including their mood, upbringing, weather, level of awareness, etc., and one of those factors is your own opinion about them. If you desire a person's behavior toward you to change, the first thing you can do is to stop contributing to the undesirable behavior through your negative opinions (or through negative speech like complaint or gossip). The vibes you project onto someone or something get reflected back in their relationship to you. Take for instance animals or plants: when you project positive feelings or thoughts onto them, they reflect back your positivity; when you project thoughts of fear or hate, they respond accordingly. If it's true for plants and animals, it's even more so with humans.

When you harbor love in your heart, it transforms all other feelings, and it is love that gets radiated to anyone you think about or talk about. Upon returning to love, your opinion about the person changes and you'll clearly see that they are not a nasty abuser but rather a victim of circumstances who is hurt and confused themselves; lacking the ability to heal or change, they're merely behaving in an unskillful manner. Any former misunderstanding gets cleared up and a feeling of compassion will arise toward them.

Still trapped in your head space, mentally judging and criticizing the person, any mental prayer or a verbal request to the person concerned would be ineffective. Returning to love puts you in touch with a power that has an ability to heal and transform anything it touches. When you feel the love flow through you strongly, visualize the person in your spiritual heart center and pray to their true Self to bring about healing and transformation so that they may return to their true nature of love.

*"Oh true Self, you are an ocean of infinite love,*

*You are the true abode of our hearts.*

*Shower upon [Insert name of the person] your nectar of grace,*

*And melt all walls of separation from the loving space.*

*Please bring healing and closure to [name of person]'s mind,*

*And let their heart experience constant love."*

Keep praying for love for yourself and the person concerned until the feeling of love inside you becomes so strong that it melts away any residual hurtful emotion. Keep sending love to that person and you'll notice that it increases the influx of love into your own heart. This is a powerful practice that will bring harmony and healing to all your relationships.

When two people harbor disharmonious thoughts about each other, it creates an atmosphere of emotional turbulence which clouds clear thinking. It dams the free flow of love to and from the spiritual heart center which results in buildup of tension in the body and a feeling of heaviness in the chest. Surrendering your thoughts and praying for love enables you to clear up this blockage. Prayer enables you to knock a few holes in the dam to let some love trickle in; as you keep letting go of thoughts and keep sending and receiving love, the holes widen and allow more love to flow through. Eventually the flow of love becomes so strong that it brings down the dam completely and dissolves all tension from within, returning lightness to your being, and clarity to your mind. You will feel the relief of being reestablished in the heart space of love and the solution will become apparent from there.

The realization will dawn in you that what matters most is returning to feeling this love in your heart. Everything else is secondary. A heart devoid of love can never experience true contentment no matter how much you pamper it with riches or adoration. When you lack love, you could have everything, but it may still feel like nothing; in the presence of love, you may have nothing, but you will feel like the King of the universe. You will realize that love is supreme, and with every conflict that shuts you out of love, your yearning to return to it becomes stronger. A day will arrive when you will become so firmly established in love that nothing will be able to shake you out of it. You will happily sacrifice even your own ego to retain communion with the love within. The same thoughts which created strong urges in you to fight and to insist on having it your way will lose power over you in the presence of love. All thoughts disappear even before they appear and will leave you in deep blissful *Samadhi*. The interesting side-effect of this is that once you lose interest in competing and become a lover instead of a fighter, the external world will happily offer you the things that were denied to you when you used to fight for them!

"The more you fly from *Prakruti*, the more she follows you; and if you do not care for her at all, she becomes your slave." – Swami Vivekananda

After this, if needed or if the situation calls for it, you may even engage the person in a discussion. You can say the following sample prayer prior to the meeting (in addition to the prayer above).

*"Oh true Self, you are an ocean of infinite love,*

*You are the true abode of my heart.*

*I love you, and my wish is to be in constant communion with you.*

*Please remove any obstacles that prevent the flow of love to and from my heart.*

*Please give me the strength to speak in such a manner that it brings healing and closure to the mind of [insert name of person]."*

When you sincerely pray and feel love for someone, even if no external change is to be noticed initially, you will still experience deep inner peace and harmony independent of outside circumstances. As you stay rooted in this harmonious feeling within, eventually it will manifest in your external circumstances as well. The resolution may come in unexpected forms. Don't expect the outcome to take a particular shape; otherwise you risk slipping from the loving heart into the judgmental head. Just stay rooted in the feeling of love and flow in the direction it takes you. The outcome may be better than you ever imagined.

Love is such a powerful language that it can reach the hearts of others even when all verbal attempts to communicate have failed. When you encounter someone who is either being hurtful toward you, toward someone else or even toward themselves (or has been in the past), before giving them verbal advice or engaging them in a discussion, consider praying for love and healing for them. Upon offering a prayer and feeling love for them, if you speak to them, the words will flow beautifully and will surely bring about a harmonious resolution.

This procedure of praying for love to bring about harmony can also be applied to relationships with children. Since children have more malleable minds than adults, prayers work even more effectively on them. If you find your child to be misbehaving consistently, despite your repeated pleas and admonitions, check your inner state. Pray for love for yourself and the child. Visualize the image of the child as you feel the love strongly in your spiritual heart center. It will heal you both of any ill feelings or emotional upset generated from any previous interactions. Any communication you have with your child from that loving space will bring about a resolution that is seldom brought about by any amount of scolding or punishment. Again, the resolution may come in unexpected ways. Maybe it's not the child's behavior that needs to change, but your attitude toward them. When water nourishes a plant, it doesn't demand the plant grow into a certain shape; it just gives unconditionally. Love doesn't seek to control; love frees. The plant will grow into whatever shape it's destined to as long as it's given loving space and nourishment. Yes, tough love and discipline may sometimes be needed until a child reaches a certain age, but even that is effective only when you're internally grounded in the loving heart, not in the anxious mind. In the presence of love, your relationship will bloom into full flower. Be love now; your dear ones will be grateful.

## Key #9: Learn to Laugh

Develop the habit of reading a few clean jokes every day until you get a hearty laugh. After a few days of doing this, as your body develops the habit of laughing, you will find yourself breaking into fits of laughter in situations that formerly used to trigger stress. Laughter brings you back to the feeling of joy; and joy is just another name for love. Don't take life too seriously. Take it easy. The worst thing that can happen is you losing your cool and forgetting who you really are. Whenever something goes "wrong," instead of blaming someone or yourself, just have a good laugh (but not at the expense of others) and return to Love.

\*\*\*

In addition to the nine keys mentioned above, there are a few other keys like non-insistence, non-interference, etc., are touched upon in "Chapter XXII: The Four Principles of Love." You need not memorize any of these, but slow and repeated reading, especially at times of conflict or misunderstanding, may be helpful. The main thing you need to do is return to love as quickly as possible whenever you feel you are slipping away from it (also see "Chapter XII: The process of Returning to Love"). Returning to and abiding in that true nature of love will enable the natural goodness in you to flow and heal your relationship with others and restore harmony and peace within and without.

# Chapter XXI

## Rise Above the Illusion of Pleasure

"Let me tell you what the body is like. Whatever pleasure it gave in youth, it will give an equivalent amount of pain in one's old age. He says, 'This is my body,' but it produces suffering even when he pampers it as his own. The teeth are brushed and polished, and yet they bring pain and suffering. The eyes hurt, the ears hurt and everything torments. That, which is your own, torments you. Such is the worldly life..." - Dadashri

"People find this world a beautiful and a harmonious place. But really it is a factory of death. Death is inevitable with old age. Whatever spiritual work you accomplish in this life will be your own and yours to keep." - Dadashri

\*\*\*

The soul has no needs. The soul is full and complete in itself. When we rest in our true Self, either in deep sleep or through deep meditation, we rest in its abode of infinite love, peace and joy in deep contentment of being with no needs whatsoever.

Our body on the other hand has several needs. The moment we wake up into this body from sleep or meditation, we are reminded that the body needs to be taken care of: washed, cleaned, purged, fed, entertained and pampered. And since the body is aware of its own mortality, it wishes to propagate itself through its offspring, and for that it demands sex.

Just as a baby cries out to get attention from her mother when she's hungry, the body sends out distress signals like thirst, hunger, bowel movements, pain, loneliness, boredom, arousal, etc., whenever it seeks attention to fulfill its various needs. The mind through these distress signals (urges) and "thoughts" constantly bring to our attention: what to do, what not to do, etc., in order to minimize pain and maximize pleasure, prevent threats to the body, attend to its needs and increase the odds of the body's survival.

When we lose ourselves in our mind in a constant stream of thoughts related to the body and its needs and fears, we lose touch with our true identity as the soul, a self-content and blissful being, and lose ourselves in this false identity of body filled with inadequacy and fear.

To be drawn away from its true home, an abode of love, joy and abundance, into this pitiful state of a body with its constant struggle for existence and constant competition for procreation is a painful and traumatic experience for the soul.

When the needs of the body are met, the mind calms down for some time, allowing the soul to briefly experience the peace and joy of resting in itself. This is only a temporary interval before the mind becomes active again, generating worrisome thoughts and painful distress signals reminding you to tend to the needs of the body yet again. And the cycle continues...

The only peace you experience is after one need is met and before another begins. The mind misinterprets these brief intervals between pains as pleasure, and seeks more and more pleasure by continued indulgence in sensual gratification of the body. But such misguided adventure seldom leads to lasting peace.

"Even if the object of your enjoyment were to be suddenly available in abundance, it still cannot give you lasting pleasure; the pleasure will soon turn into boredom! Then you will wonder 'Why is it that the same experience that I craved for so much, and gave me so much pleasure when I first tasted it, doesn't fulfill me anymore?' It is because there was no inherent pleasure in the object in the first place. The pleasure you perceived was an illusionary pleasure that existed only in relation to pain. Pleasure is a state of high that is felt only in relation to a low, pain. The intensity of pleasure that you felt upon attaining an object was proportional to the intensity of thirst for that object (pain in the form of longing). Quenching of that thirst, or ending of that pain, is what you perceived as pleasure. In the absence of pain (thirst or longing), the same objects are incapable of providing you with any pleasure and hence become boring. You might seek more stimuli (increasing your thirst, thus increasing pain) to experience an even more intense high, to feel more pleasure. But eventually the instrument (the body) through which you enjoy the object would age and wear out to the point that you would be unable to sense any higher degree of pleasure, no matter how much extra stimuli you provide. The memory of pleasure from previous enjoyment will create a longing that can no longer be fulfilled, creating pain. As much pleasure as you enjoyed in the presence of the object, an equal amount of pain will you have to suffer when you lose the object of enjoyment or the ability to enjoy it." – Yogi Kanna, *Nirvana: Absolute Freedom*

Flowing with the river of love, your true Self, is the only source of true contentment and peace. Any sense of pleasure derived from the non-self or external objects is an illusion that exists only in relation to pain. Such pursuit of illusory pleasure is like seeking to quench your thirst by chasing mirages. It only leads to more pain and frustration.

The basic needs of the body have to be met for obvious reasons, but to focus your life on pleasuring yourself by over-indulging in the needs of the body is to embark on a failing mission that only results in increasing greed, discontent and pain.

"After the unbearable heat of the day, why is it that the cattle soak in the dirty muddy waters? The deep desire for coolness from heat makes them forget the stench of the dirty muddy water. Similarly modern day humans who suffer from the constant struggles and tensions of daily life at work and at home, seek a diversion from the fire of such tensions and a release through sex and forget its consequences over and over again." – *Dadashri*

Unable to find clean waters, the cattle soak in muddy waters to escape from the heat of the sun. Similarly, when your attention is occupied by constant worries over the needs of the body, you lose touch with your true Self, the abode of love (clean water) and seek temporary relief from the heat of suffering through sex and such pleasures (muddy waters). However, as we have already seen, pleasure is pleasure only when it follows pain. Without pain, it doesn't take long for pleasure to transform into boredom. In the pursuit of this illusory pleasure, we forget the Self and choose to return to suffering, life after life.

Of the various needs of the body that are misused for entertainment and escape, the one that humans obsess most with is the need for a sexual partner. Lost in the pursuit of sex, humans forget the happiness of the soul and get lost in a world of loneliness and suffering. Hence among the various pleasures pursued by humans, sex merits a special mention. It is worth looking at what happens when we use sex just for recreation in casual relationships rather than for procreation within a committed relationship.

The act of sex establishes a special bond between the couple. This connection is created on a physical, emotional and astral plane every time two people have intercourse. Upon having sex with someone you will be able to sense their thoughts and emotions more easily. This was designed by the universe so that the parents of a child born out of this sexual intercourse can understand each other and care for the child in a better way. Earlier, we saw how the experience of one body and one mind is itself a distressing experience for a soul. So, relationships are even more complex for the soul since it now has to cater to the needs of two bodies and two minds!

Often when people set out to seek a sexual partner, the impulse is usually driven by a feeling of lack. They feel incomplete without a partner. People sense a void within themselves, which they hope to fill with a partner (or just with the act of sex). But can two unhappy and needy individuals come together and form a happy and content couple? Very unlikely, isn't it? In the heat of passion, they might temporarily forget their individual lack and unhappiness and enjoy a temporary illusion of happiness. They can build a wall around themselves and feel cozy and comfortable in their dream world. However, their minds will soon remind them of the real sources of their unhappiness, and bring them back to earth soon after the honeymoon period on cloud nine is over. Thus relationships sought on a purely physical level, coming from a place of lack, often end in more lack.

On the other hand, relationships can result in true harmony and joy if both souls who come together are devoted toward returning home to their true Self and they combine their energies in this task leading to ultimate harmony. But when sex is used just for recreation as an escape from the constant stream of compulsive thinking or to seek relief from boredom, it leads to a lot of complications. Even after the couple splits up physically after the sex act, the resulting emotional and mental connection between the couple remains in the astral plane. It usually takes at least nine months of no sexual activity for this connection to dissolve. [If a child is born as a result of the sexual act, the connection can last for the entire lifetime; however, it can be dissolved through spiritual practice.] If either of the persons have sex in the next nine months, even if it is with a different person, this connection between the couple becomes more strongly established. Hence, after the person has had sex with a second person, he or she is not only astrally connected with the body-mind of this new person, but also with that of the former lover. Thus with every sexual relationship, a new bond gets established and the person accumulates a baggage of karmic astral connections.

If experience of one body and mind can be distressing for the soul, imagine how distressing it would be for a soul to be connected to the bodies and minds of so many different people. Additionally, if many of the former lovers are suffering from heartbreak, resentment and jealousy because of the resulting break-ups, the person will be able to sense all their painful emotions and thoughts through this astral connection. This accumulated emotional and mental baggage can be really overwhelming in a person who indulges in casual sex with multiple partners. They may find themselves becoming suddenly depressed for no reason. Often people try to numb this emotional and mental pain by using drugs, alcohol, food or more sex. However, numbing these emotions or suppressing them does not make them go away.

In order to truly heal from this emotional pain and trauma, one needs to adopt a lifestyle of *Brahmacharya*, the way of Love.

\*\*\*

When you have love in your heart, you lack nothing, for love overflows inside as abundant joy and bliss.

When you have love in your heart, you fear nothing, for love transforms everything it touches into love.

Wherever there is lack and fear, Love is not.

Thoughts of lack often arise in the head space, inviting you to abandon the abundance of the heart space.

When such needy thoughts appear in your head, telling you that you are incomplete without something or someone, pause, notice and invite love in.

Release such thoughts as soon as they appear into the river of love.

Just as darkness leaves at the arrival of light, lack and fear depart as soon as you flow with love.

When you meet others from this place of love, you relate to them from a place of contentment, joy and peace and bring harmony and friendship into every relationship.

Flowing with the river of love will take you to the ocean of supreme love-bliss, *Brahman*.

So the lifestyle of one who constantly chooses love over lack is called *Brahmacharya*.

\*\*\*

It typically takes 9 months of no sexual activity (including masturbation) combined with daily meditation to heal the emotional pains and dissolve the astral connections from past relationships completely. This is accomplished not through force or suppression, but by flowing with love, through *Brahmacharya*.

There is no suppression in *Brahmacharya*. The energy that is normally used to feed negative thinking and the pursuit of illusory pleasures is now redirected toward meditation and healthier *Sattvic* habits that encourage abidance in the Self. Whenever thoughts of lack arise in your mind, simply release those thoughts from your headspace without any judgment or guilt, and keep returning to love in your heart space. *Brahmacharya* is the best aid to spiritual progress. It will heal you from the inside out and open the flood gates for more love to flow in.

Healthy *Sattvic* habits like meditation, healthy food and exercise are generally harder to cultivate in the beginning compared to unhealthy *Rajasic* and *Tamasic* habits. However, if you persist with *sattvic* habits long-term, they will lead you to a place of true contentment, peace and health. This is explained in the verses below from the *Bhagavad Gita*:

"And now hear from Me, O lord of the *Bharatas*, of the threefold pleasure, in which one delights by practice and surely comes to the end of pain."

"That which is like poison at first, like nectar at the end, that pleasure is declared to be *Sattvic*, born of purity of one's own mind."

"That pleasure which arises from the contact of the sense-organ with the object, at first like nectar, in the end like poison, that is declared to be *Rajasic*."

"That pleasure which at first and in the sequel is delusive of the self, arising from sleep, indolence, and heedlessness, that pleasure is declared to be *Tamasic*." - Bhagavad Gita 18:36-18:39

As you cultivate *sattvic* habits with patience and persistence, the painful emotional charge within will gradually dissipate and the astral connections that got created from unhealthy relationships will heal and dissolve. As a result, your soul will gradually be able to rest in its true abode of love, peace and joy.

Consider experimenting with nine months of *Brahmacharya*. You will come to discover its benefits on your own and make up your mind as to whether such a lifestyle is indeed for you or not. However, if you get scared by the initial challenges and withdrawal symptoms that you face by adopting any *sattvic* lifestyle and give up prematurely, you will never discover the treasures that come from persisting with it. During these nine months it is also helpful to eat food prepared at home, as food is often charged with the thought vibrations of the person who prepares it and will affect the mind of the person who eats it. Hence, observing *Brahmacharya* will be easier when the food is prepared at home yourself or by people with similar goals. Preferably eat food that is easy to digest composed of fresh fruits, vegetables and whole grains. Try to avoid use of onion, garlic, potatoes, hot spices and excess salt to help preserve the *sattvic* (harmonious) quality of food. Eating *sattvic* food prepared at home will promote inner peace and abidance in love and reduce unnecessary thoughts and distracting urges; this will help deepen your meditation.

During the *Brahmacharya* practice, you will also notice the enormous amount of effort that normally goes into seeking validation from others and attracting the opposite sex (or the same sex if you are gay). The way you dress, the way you smile, the things you buy, the way you carry yourself, the company you seek, the things you say, etc., can all be traced to the intent of attracting attention of others or wanting something from others.

"The moment you 'want' something from others, you surrender the 'remote control' of your life into their hands. You are now at the mercy of the other for providing you with what you 'want.' You try to cater to others who can give you the thing you want, be it money, approval, attention, appreciation, respect, sex, entertainment, etc. You are afraid of disapproval, and fear that the other may withhold from you what you think you 'want' from them. You trade your freedom and integrity and change yourself to suit other people's expectations so that they will approve of you and give you what you seek. With this loss of freedom begins the downward spiral that leads to loss of joy and loss of peace." – Yogi Kanna, *Nirvana: Absolute Freedom*

Life doesn't have to be this complicated. When you turn to the love of the Self, instead of seeking love from others, life becomes much simpler and much more abundant and fulfilling.

Minimize your needs and economize your time and energy so that you are spending less time catering to the needs of the body-mind and more time in meditation, radiating and receiving love to and from your true Self, the source of infinite love.

"To come to know, experience, and live in Infinite-Eternal-Awareness-Love-Bliss is definitely worth the time spent practicing."

"You'll discover you're not a body living in a world."

"You are eternal awareness, perfect love-joy."

The above quotes are from the book *"The Most Direct Means to Eternal Bliss"* by Michael Langford. (Chapter 8, Verses 161-163)

Life becomes a constant communion with your true Self which overflows as the river of love in your heart. Very little is then needed for the daily maintenance of the body. You see the body as a vehicle to help you return to your true source, not as a shaky home that you need to hold onto and constantly worry about.

Having experienced the nightmare of falsely identifying with the inadequacy in the body, we realize the true worth of returning home to our true identity of our true Self, the ocean of Love. The drop gets carried by the river of love in our heart and merges back into the ocean of supreme love.

The circle completes itself.

Rise above the illusion of pleasure. Choose the way of love, choose *Brahmacharya*, and it will take you home.

# Chapter XXII

## Four Principles of Love

When you invite love into your heart, life becomes really simple. There is no need to read hundreds of books or attend thousands of lectures. All you need is to connect with the love in your heart, and it will guide you home to true fulfillment and joy. If we had to put this simple principle into words, we would call it the "Principle of love."

The principle of love is very simple. Whenever you are in doubt about whether your thoughts, speech or actions are leading you in the right direction, just notice your spiritual heart; see if harboring this thought, speech or action is causing your heart to open up allowing more love in, or causing your heart to shut down pushing love away. Just ask yourself, "What will love do now?" and simply flow in the direction of love.

If more guidance is needed, we can say that the principle of love has four derivatives. Let's call them "The Four Principles of Love." They are:

## Principle 1: Honor your truth

**Know your truth:** Know your heart's true desire and honor it.

**Live your truth:** Be honest to yourself, and live your truth. Don't engage in something to please others or to seek approval, appreciation or validation. Don't engage in something even to please your own ego which only cares about instant gratification and not about long-term consequences. Engage in something because it is aligned with your heart's true desire, your truth. Only your true Self cares about you, and when you live your truth by following the love in your heart, it will lead you to your true Self, the abode of true fulfillment and joy.

**Speak your truth:** Be honest to others, and speak your truth. Practice the art of saying "no" to other people (lovingly) and to your "own" thoughts (firmly) when invited to participate in things that don't align with your truth. Don't try to change yourself for others. Be authentic, kind and considerate to yourself as well as to others.

## Principle 2: Honor another's truth

**Non-Judgment:** Your path need not be the best path for others. Honor other people's choices and paths just as you would want them to honor yours. Refrain from passing judgment about others. If you notice thoughts of judgment happening, simply notice them, release them and return to love.

**Non-criticism:** Be non-critical of other people's beliefs and practices. Remember: "If you have nothing good to say, don't say anything at all."

**Non-interference:** Don't give advice unless specifically asked for it. Even when asked for, try to give it in the form of metaphors and self-deprecating stories and examples instead of direct advice, so that the other person does not feel inferior in any way.

**Non-insistence:** Don't insist on having it your way. Go with the flow. Adjust everywhere and avoid clashes. Practice of non-insistence makes your inner state independent of external circumstances and makes it easier to preserve outer harmony even with the most challenging people.

"There is no truth in this world that is worth insisting upon. Anything that is insisted upon is not the truth at all!" – Dadashri

Try this experiment suggested by *Pujyashree* Deepakbhai Desai, disciple of Dadashri: Pick one day and simply remain a witness for the entire day as you go about your daily activities. Just go with the flow of things without interfering with anyone or anything for the entire day and see what happens. Receive what is given, do what is told, listen to what is spoken, love what happens. Try this for just one day. Notice the tendency of the ego to insist and interfere through mind, speech and action at various points in the day. It may claim "This HAS to be done this way. If it is not done 'my' way, the world will not run properly." Just try this experiment of non-insistence for one day and see how smoothly and harmoniously the world runs when you flow with love instead of insisting or interfering with your ego.

**Noble Silence and Deep Listening:** Refrain from talking about your path or beliefs when not asked, and especially to those who are not interested. Each person has different beliefs and practices, and talking about your beliefs may trigger an argument or debate leading to ill will in the other person. Always seek to preserve peace even when provoked, by observing noble silence. If you have to say something, you can say: "Yes, you are right from your viewpoint," and truly mean it when you say it. Don't try to preach or to correct other people; each person will learn their own lessons from their own unique experience. So just remain humble like a student and observe noble silence. Try to ensure that the words that come out of your mouth are "True, kind, helpful and brief."

## Principle 3: Abide in Love, Be content in Love

Love is your natural state, your home. Abiding in love, your true home, brings you the greatest fulfillment. When you visit any place as a guest, you may feel entertained and excited for a time, but after a while you will start missing home. Similarly, whenever you choose to embody anything less than pure love, it will trigger a stressful feeling inside your heart as a gentle reminder, "Come back home, my child." Spend enough time in meditation or prayer during the day abiding in the heart space as love. You will experience true contentment and will observe that your inner state is completely independent of external circumstances. You will be able to remain in a state of joy, lightness and ease within even when faced with the toughest challenges on the outside. When you flow with the river of love, you will be able to flow around the hardest obstacles with ease and grace. Even if faced with physical death it won't take away from your joy as you will only see it as an opportunity to reunite with the Ocean of love. Spend enough time abiding in pure love.

## Principle 4: Keep returning to Love

Whenever you feel out of place and find yourself experiencing or radiating anything other than pure love, ask yourself: "What will love do now?" Read the entire book again and master the art and science of returning to love. Your heart will thank you.

# Chapter XXIII

## Guided Meditation - Being a Loving Presence

Provided below is a transcript for guided meditation practice. You may want to record the instructions on a tape or CD and play it back on an audio device (Note: Please do not practice this meditation while driving a vehicle or while operating machinery). A 20-minute audio track titled "Guided Meditation and Deep Relaxation" is available for purchase through the website: www.yogikanna.com (it is also available through iTunes, Amazon and other online retailers).

On the first day you can start by meditating for 20 minutes, twice a day (or at least once a day). Gradually increase the length of your meditation session by one minute a day. If you do this, by the 40th day you will be sitting in meditation 60 minutes a session, twice a day. Going forward, maintain at least that level of practice. Meanwhile, the author highly recommends reading the book *"The Most Direct*

*Means to Eternal Bliss"* by Michael Langford. That book contains detailed instructions on meditation practices which in the author's experience are the most direct way to get in touch with your true Self. (The instructions come directly from a liberated sage and hence are much more powerful, a form of direct transmission.) The book also contains detailed instructions on how to avoid common pitfalls and detours on the way to final liberation. More about that book is mentioned in the next section, "Recommended Reading and Resources."

\*\*\*

Below is the instruction for the Guided meditation Practice "Being a Loving Presence"

There are three parts to this meditation:

1. Relaxation
2. Letting go of effort
3. Becoming one with the loving spaciousness

## Part 1: Relaxation

Sit or lie down in a comfortable position.

Keep your eyes initially open.

Just let all things be exactly as they are.

Close your eyes (not while you read this chapter :). When you do the actual practice by replaying these instructions or by following the audio track from www.yogikanna.com, you will need to keep your eyes closed for the entire meditation).

Consciously relax your whole body, from head to toe.

Relax and release any tension you may feel, as you run your attention through your body.

Relax the crown of your head by allowing the scalp muscles to relax.

Relax your eyebrows; release any tension you feel between your eyebrows.

Relax the muscles in your forehead.

Relax the little muscles under your eyes.

Allow your cheek muscles to relax.

Relax your neck, allowing your head to balance freely on the top of your spine, and imagine the crown of your head piercing through the sky.

Gently relax your shoulders, allowing them to widen.

Gently allow the relaxation to flow down into your arms, relaxing your elbows, forearms, wrists and fingers.

Relax each individual finger on your hands, one by one.

Relax your shoulders.

Let the wave of relaxation flow down your back, relaxing your shoulder blades, your upper and lower back.

Relax your chest, your stomach and abdominal muscles.

Notice that you are breathing.

Relax your hips, your glutes. Feel yourself comfortably seated (or lying) on your chair or cushion.

Let the relaxation slowly flow down your legs, relaxing your glutes, your thighs, your quads, all the way down to your knees.

Relax those knees. Let the relaxation flow down further into your legs, into your shins and calf muscles all the way to your feet.

Relax your feet.

Allow the relaxation to flow down into your feet, relaxing your ankles and your toes.

Feel your whole body completely relaxed from head to toe.

There is nothing to do, nowhere to go, except to be exactly where you are.

Just let go, and relax.

## Part 2: Letting go of effort

Notice how relaxed you are.

Let go of all effort.

Relax and release all effort.

Effortlessly notice your inner space.

Notice that you are conscious.

Notice how it takes no effort to remain conscious.

Keep noticing your inner space effortlessly,

and allow your attention to rest anywhere in your body, wherever it feels comfortable.

Just relax and keep noticing your inner space.

If you notice any feelings or emotions arising in this space of consciousness, make no effort to change those feelings or emotions.

Let them be exactly as they are.

Make no effort to change anything.

Notice the space in which these feelings arise.

Let go, and relax into that space.

Rest there, effortlessly.

Just keep letting go of effort, and allow yourself to rest into this sense of spaciousness.

Keep noticing this spaciousness within.

If you notice that you are thinking, make no effort to complete those thoughts.

Let go of thoughts as they arise.

Let go of thoughts even before they arise.

Relax and release all effort.

Notice the space in which thoughts arise.

Let go, and relax into that space.

Rest there,

Remain there, effortlessly.

Keep noticing your inner space.

If you notice any restlessness, boredom or discomfort, make no effort to change those feelings.

Let them be exactly as they are.

Notice the space in which those feelings arise.

Let go, and relax into that space.

Remain there, effortlessly.

## Part 3: Becoming one with loving spaciousness

Keep noticing your inner space.

Let go of any visual idea of having a body.

Allow your inner space to merge with the outer space.

Expand into the feeling of spaciousness, consciousness, beingness.

There is nothing to do, nowhere to go except to be exactly where you are.

Rest in the feeling of spaciousness, allowing everything to be exactly as they are.

Feel the ocean of love within and without, embracing everything that arises.

Whatever arises in this vast space of consciousness, just notice the space in which it arises.

Let go and relax into that space.

Thoughts, emotions and sensations arise and subside in consciousness just as clouds appear and disappear in the sky.

So just be a loving presence, letting things appear and disappear; neither resisting, nor holding onto anything.

Let everything get consumed into your ocean of loving consciousness.

Dive deeper into the ocean of love.

Become one with the ocean of love.

Bask in the joy of this communion.

\*\*\*

# Chapter XXIV

## Commitment to Awakening True Wisdom

A boy accompanied his father to a river bed one day. His father told him: "Son, there are lots of stones on the shore of this river. Many are just cheap stones, but a few of them are precious gems. See if you can find any precious gems; it might be your lucky day!" After learning from his father how to differentiate a precious gem from a regular stone, the boy went looking for them. He would pick up a stone, inspect it, and if it happened to be just another regular stone, he would toss it into the flowing river. He kept picking up one stone after another, and kept tossing them into the river. After going through a few dozen stones, he almost gave up hope of finding anything valuable but continued looking. Soon he picked up a shiny precious stone. It was a perfectly shaped gem, but before the realization dawned on him, his hand out of habit tossed it into the flowing river! He watched with his own eyes how the precious gem he had picked up got lost among other stones and sucked underneath the stream of the river. "Oh my god, what have I done? Why did I throw that? It was one of those precious stones that I was looking for." His father, who was watching from a distance, smiled at him and said, "Son, that's what happens when you mindlessly pick up one thing after another. Sometimes you may find something really precious, but if you don't give careful consideration to it, and move on to the next thing in a hurry, it may be too late before you realize the true worth of what came to you. From now on, carefully inspect what comes your way before you decide to let go of it and move on to the next. You never know when the next precious thing will come into your hand. So be mindful."

Like the boy in the story above, there are many among us who pick up one book after another hoping to find something of value. But often we don't give enough time and consideration to experimenting with the practices and solutions proposed in the book. Many of these might indeed be commonplace books offering cheap entertainment, but sometimes we will come across a precious gem that really inspires us. Before we let the inspiration set in and become a transformational insight, we have already gone on to the next book! By the time we finish reading the new book, any inspiration obtained from the previous book may have disappeared, leaving us in the same place as before we opened the first page. Any opportunity to gain something of value from a good book is lost when we mindlessly go on to the next one without giving the current book enough time and consideration. Worse, it may leave us with more noise in our head, because we will have picked up impractical knowledge instead of practical wisdom.

There is a distinction between Knowledge and Wisdom. Knowledge is of external things that can be known (knowledge of things, people, events, etc.), whereas wisdom is to know the knower: Self-knowledge. Once you know your true Self and gain wisdom, there is stillness, peace and fulfillment within; whereas excess knowledge (of things that can be known) only increases the noise in your mind.

Excess knowledge, unlike wisdom, increases pride and egotism, which eventually leads to greed, envy and suffering.

It is only through personal experience that you gain wisdom. No one can give it to you, not even books written on that subject. Books are like maps; they can point you in a certain direction. But it's up to you to physically go on the trip, to try different directions that have been suggested, and see for yourself the true consequences of those choices. The firsthand experience resulting from actually traveling the path suggested by the maps awakens the wisdom within you. Mere reading of books with a view to accumulate information in your brain leads to impractical knowledge.

If you found this book to be any inspiration at all, consider spending more time with it before you move on. Just as you learn more from a long-term committed relationship than from a casual fling, you will get a lot more from studying and experimenting with the message of a book than from reading it just once rapidly. Reading a book is like looking at a cookbook which contains descriptions and pictures of various food items; if you actually want to eat the food, you need to physically cook it according to the instructions in the book; merely reading the cookbook and thinking of food is not enough to satisfy your hunger. The main purpose of this book is to inspire you on your journey to Self-realization, and point out the tools and resources the author himself found useful. Mere inspiration is not enough; you need to actually use the tools and explore the suggested practices if you wish to satisfy your spiritual yearning and experience the bliss of the Self first hand. Several pointers, meditations and prayers have been described in earlier chapters of the book; putting them into practice will allow you to experience the coolness of your soul, and give you the necessary conviction, inspiration and clarity to jump-start your journey of Self-discovery. Still, to tackle all obstacles that come in the way of permanent realization of the Self, you need precise directions. In the next section, I am going to direct you to a few books and resources that will offer you just that. It may sound a bit contradictory to my earlier advice discouraging reading of one book after another; however, the books that I am about to suggest in the section to follow, especially the first one, *The Most Direct Means to Eternal Bliss* (and it may be the only one you need!), won't distract you from the path; indeed, they are practical guides to help you progress further on the same path. The book you hold in your hands is great for giving you the inspiration and tools needed to get started on the direct path to self-realization, and you can read it as many times as you need to that end. But to progress further on the path, you need the book(s) suggested in the next section. The first two books suggested in the following chapter are written by liberated sages (unlike this book that's written by a practitioner).

A practitioner is someone who has successfully knocked a hole in the wall that separates him from the garden of love. Occasionally he's able to stick his hand or head into the hole and enjoy the cool breeze and scenery of the garden; but he's unable to enter the garden yet and must soon get back to work chipping away at the wall. His descriptions of the garden (such as in this book) can only be as complete as the size and narrow angle of the hole allow him to see. A liberated sage, on the other hand, is someone who has successfully torn down the entire wall and lives in the garden of love. He has a three-hundred-and-sixty degree view of the garden and can also give you the tools he himself used to tear down the wall to get there. He knows every obstacle he faced in the process and can offer you exact guidance on how to overcome it. Yet the best teacher is useless if the student lacks the desire to learn. The first purpose of the present book is to reach out to your heart, rekindle the love and remind you of your true home. Once that homing instinct awakens strongly in your heart, you can to proceed to the next step by picking up the tools provided in the next section, and get to work on tearing down the wall that separates you from the garden of love. This is the second purpose of this book: to point you to the tools and teachings that actually work, since there exist a million that don't. After that you need not return to this book again. When you successfully knock a small hole in the wall and see the garden of love with your own eyes, your conviction becomes strong and the light of love emanating from the garden itself guides you further. But until that desire to return to your true home becomes strong enough to convince you that the path you have chosen is indeed the one to take you there, the slow and repeated reading of this book, combined with daily spiritual practice, can be very helpful.

If this book touched your heart in a positive way, consider committing more time to it until a strong desire to return home to the sanctuary of love awakens in your heart. Also consider recommending or gifting this book to others you think may resonate with the message it contains. You are also welcome to write an honest heartfelt review of the book to help other readers discover it. Best wishes and much love!

# Chapter XXV

## Recommended Reading and Resources

"Only he who has attained immortal life can save the world. For the ignorant one to help another is but the blind leading the blind." – *Sri Ramana Maharshi*

\*\*\*

The author of this book is neither a spiritual teacher nor an awakened sage. The author is a practitioner who is devoted to the love of the true Self, and through this book is playing the role of a messenger. This book is written with the intent of serving as a signpost and inspiration to people who wish to liberate themselves from suffering and live in absolute contentment, joy and peace.

There are very few authentic and fully awakened sages who have revealed the direct path teachings for those who aspire to spiritual liberation. Opening your heart to their teachings is the most direct means to liberation. However, these teachings are not easy to find as they are buried among the many distractions and detours being taught in the name of spirituality. After spending more than fifteen years exploring and practicing various teachings, the author found the ones listed below to be the most helpful and direct in the journey to permanent release from suffering.

If Self-realization or liberation is what you truly desire, and if the author had to recommend just one book to you, it would be *"The Most Direct Means to Eternal Bliss"* by Michael Langford. That book contains the essence of all spiritual teachings in existence as well as detailed step-by-step instructions to help one abide in one's true Self, the abode of infinite love-bliss. It is an instruction manual for enlightenment and a special gift to humanity from your true Self. Some of the practices described in the book are: The Awareness Watching Awareness Method, The Abandon Release Method, The Eternal Method, The Infinite Space Method, The Loving All Method and The Loving Consciousness Method. The instructions are simple, direct and powerful. The author of this book (*Return to Love*) practices the meditation methods as described in *The*

*Most Direct Means to Eternal Bliss* and recommends it to anyone who is desirous of final liberation. The proof is in the pudding. If the title sounds too promising, consider practicing the teachings as described in the book sincerely and observe the results for yourself.

If you seek additional inspiration, the author recommends reading quotes by awakened sages from the past. A word of warning, however: An awakened sage is like a mirror, and his answer to any question reflects the needs of the particular consciousness level of the questioner. Usually the answer is perfect for the questioner, though it may not be the right answer for a person at a different level. If the answer is generalized for the masses, the intellect can misinterpret it and cause confusion. Thus, if a bunch of questions asked by questioners at different levels are grouped together in a book, many answers may seem contradictory, although the sage's original teaching is totally free of contradiction. This contradiction can be resolved, however, if the questions and answers are interpreted by another Awakened sage. The book *"The Seven Steps to*

*Awakening*," is such a compilation. It's a powerful collection of quotes by seven great sages: *Ramana Maharshi, Nisargadatta Maharaj, Sri Sadhu Om, Annamalai Swami, Muruganar, Shankara* and *Vasistha*. What makes this book truly special is that it not only contains quotes by seven different truly liberated sages, but the quotes have been selected and arranged by a fully liberated sage himself!

You can find where to purchase the two books mentioned above by visiting the website: www.thefreedomreligionpress.com.

If you are looking for ways to create peace and harmony in your day-to-day, worldly interactions with others while working on your inner spiritual growth, the author highly recommends studying the teachings of Dadashri (Please see the sub-section "Highly Recommended Books" for the list of books by Dadashri that you can start with.)

Dadashri expounded the science of *Akram-Vignan* (Effortless science of the Self) through which he offered extremely practical spiritual solutions to normal everyday worldly interactions. Here is a quote by *Dadashri* himself on *Akram Vignan:* "When this Science of *Akram Vignan* is revealed to the world, it would benefit people tremendously, because never before has such a science come forth. Nobody has previously ever placed any kind of *Gnan* in the depths of the worldly life. Nobody has really dealt with the worldly life interactions before. They have only talked about spirituality. Spirituality has never entered into the worldly life. The two have been kept separate. Here, *Akram Vignan* has placed spirituality into the very core of worldly life. A completely new scripture has arisen and it is also scientific. It can never be contradicted anywhere. But now, how can this *Akram Vignan* be revealed to this world? The world would be blessed if it were revealed!" – *Dadashri*

Dadashri often mentioned that in order to receive his teachings in their full purity, one has to study them in Gujarati, the language in which the teachings were originally recorded. The English translations may have unintentional distractions and seeming contradictions (due to the reasons mentioned earlier on pg. 199.) However, many may still benefit by studying these teachings in English.

If you feel so inclined, you may also attend the *Gnan vidhi* ceremony, which is a free offering by the current *Gnani Purush* (Living enlightened teacher) of *Akram Vignan* (the current teacher is *Pujyashree* Deepakbhai Desai.) Many have found it helpful to attend the *Gnan vidhi* regardless of the path or teaching they follow. It can light the flame of love in you if you attend with a sincere, open heart. The following is a description of *Gnan vidhi* from *Dada Bhagawan's* website:

"*Gnan-vidhi* is a scientific process to attain Self-Realization. It came through the *Gnani Purush Param Pujya Dadashri* (Shri Ambalal M. Patel., also fondly known as *Dada Bhagwan*). During *Gnan-vidhi*, the belief that 'I am this body-mind complex' is destroyed at subtlest level of the ego and the right belief that 'I am Pure Soul' and an internal awareness of 'who you truly are' is established within you by the grace of the *Gnani*. *Gnan-vidhi* is not a physical or metaphysical experience..." For more information on

*Gnan-vidhi* please look up *Dada Bhagawan's* website listed below.

http://www.dadabhagwan.org/gyan-vidhi.html

## Highly recommended books

- *The Most Direct Means to Eternal Bliss*, Michael Langford
- *Seven Steps to Awakening*, Ramana Maharshi, Nisargadatta Maharaj, Sri Sadhu Om, Annamalai Swami, Muruganar, Sri Sankara, Vasistha
- Books by Dadashri available free online: *The Science of Karma; Adjust Everywhere; Avoid Clashes; Whatever Has Happened is Justice; Fault is of the Sufferer; The Essence of All Religions.*
- *Think on These Things,* J.Krishnamurti
- *The Awakening of Intelligence,* J.Krishnamurti
- *Loving What is: Four Questions that can change your life, Byron Katie*
- *Your Mind Can Heal You, Frederick Bailes*
- *Nirvana: Absolute Freedom, Yogi Kanna*

## Other Resources for Healing Mind, Body and Spirit

Please note: the following practices are recommended as supplementary aids to meditation for preserving health of the body and mind, and are not necessary, nor directly useful for spiritual liberation.

## Safe Sun Gazing

Sun gazing is a very simple practice where you watch the Sun during safe hours (when the UV index 0 or 1 and the Sun is bright red or dark orange in color) starting at 10 seconds a day and gradually building it up to several minutes a day. Regular practice of sun gazing will help healing of mind, body and spirit and allow you to experience peace, health and joy. Do not start the sun gazing practice without reading the detailed instructions on Hira Ratan Manek's website at: www.solarhealing.com

## The Alexander Technique

In spite of the name, the Alexander Technique is not really a "technique." It is a course in self-awareness.

Often we think we are doing things a certain way, but in reality we may be doing them quite differently from the way we intend to. You may think you walk, stand and sit in a certain way. But if you were to watch yourself in a mirror or on video, you might be shocked to find how differently you carry your body. Similarly, you may think that you behave in a certain way; but if you were to ask other people, they might have a totally different perception of how you speak or treat others. Often our perceptions are distorted and the reality is quite different from how we process it through our senses. Because of this distortion, we may lack the ability to self-correct from a state of unease. If we try to "do" something about it, we may think we are heading in the direction of greater ease, but in fact we have stepped in the opposite direction. Imagine you're lost in a dark house and are trying to get out; no matter how hard you concentrate in the darkness, you risk slipping or stumbling on things because of your inability to see. Once someone flips on the light switch, you can automatically see what's in front of you and find your way out of the house. The Alexander Technique is a way to flip on the light switch and regain self-awareness, help us see things as they really are and return to our natural state.

Our natural state is not a static state but one that grows in a direction of greater ease. Imagine you are standing at the center, and toward your right is more and more ease; the further you travel in that direction, the more freedom you experience. There is no end to it; it just goes on and on toward limitless freedom. Toward your left is less and less ease; the further you travel to the left, the greater the degree of dis-ease. Our natural inclination is to move toward the right, toward greater ease, more freedom (no hidden political meaning intended). When someone's in tune with this natural state, they move with grace and poise and are a treat to watch. Young children have it. If you watch a toddler in action, you will see an erect spine, free joints and the head balancing easily on the neck. A healthy child walks and plays with a regal posture. We begin that way but over the years lose that spontaneity and ease. As we start imitating those around us, we develop poor postural habits and tendencies that make us lose touch with our natural state of ease and poise. As we lose touch with our natural state, the light within (awareness) dims, and our perceptions become distorted. The result is we get lost in a place of stress and disease, and lose the directions to return to our natural state of progressive ease. An Alexander Technique teacher employs touch and direction to help you regain conscious awareness of the way you use yourself during movement and during rest. They give you a glimpse of your natural state and awaken you from distorted perceptions. Once you regain self-awareness you can notice and undo any excess effort or habitual tendency that pulls you in a direction away from your natural state. As you remain in this awareness, it takes you in a direction of greater and greater ease, the direction of limitless freedom. Learning to rest, move and speak gracefully with awareness, with greater ease and poise, makes your everyday tasks and relationships more enjoyable. The author has personally benefited from learning and applying the Alexander Technique, and highly recommends it to the reader.

An Alexander Technique lesson is typically a one-on-one session taught in private. Each lesson is unique and catered to the needs of the particular individual, a typical lesson lasting 30-45 minutes. It generally takes 20 to 30 lessons under a qualified instructor to get a good grasp and understanding of the Alexander Technique, after which you should be able to apply the technique independently. Those who wish to find an instructor near them or learn more about the Alexander Technique can look up the AMSAT (American Society for the Alexander Technique) website: www.amsatonline.org. If you live in the San Diego area, the instructors I recommend are Alice Olsher and Rome Earle. For those in the Portland area, I recommend Christine Eidson.

## Pranayama

*Prana* means life force, and *yama* means regulation. *Pranayama* is the science of regulating the life force in the body by regulating the breath. Regular practice of *pranayama* is helpful for preserving physical health and mental peace. It is very beneficial in healing the mind, body and spirit and can be used by beginners as a supplementary aid to meditation. Pranayama is best learned in person under the direct supervision of a qualified instructor. Free

Introductory video tutorials taught by Ramdev Baba are available to watch and learn from on YouTube.

# Acknowledgements

I would like to express my heartfelt gratitude and love to all the awakened sages, spiritual teachers, saints and fellow travelers who have helped light the flame of love in this heart. I would also like to thank: M.S. Srinivasan, Karl Weiss, Martin Godfrey, Jacob Gearhart and Aparna Kamath for their help with proofreading, editing and for offering valuable critiques and suggestions toward making the book a better read; Nithya Iyer and Aparna Kamath for the cover design; Asun Phong for the Heart Chakra image on the cover; Prakash Shivshankar for technical assistance with layout of cover for the second edition of the book; as well as all my friends, family and other kind souls too numerous to name, for various kinds of help with this project and for offering their love, support, wisdom and encouragement. Finally, I would like to sincerely thank you, the reader, for picking up this book and opening your heart to it. May the flame of love continue to grow in your heart and spread to everyone around you. If the message in *Return to Love* had a positive impact on you, please consider suggesting this book to two other people you feel may resonate with its message, or consider leaving a book review online to help other people discover this book. Thank you!

# Other Works by Yogi Kanna from Kamath Publishing

## Books

- *Nirvana: Absolute Freedom*

## Audio albums

- Guided Meditation and Deep Relaxation
- Divine Chants for Peace, Joy and Healing

# Back Cover Blurb

"This book is written in the language of Love, a language that transcends all boundaries, nationalities and religions and speaks directly to the heart of the human soul. This book is for everyone who seeks peace of mind, healing of the heart and re-connection with the joy of their soul. If you have found this book, or if this book has found you, consider picking it up and opening your heart to it. The words in this book are not meant for your mind to accumulate as new information; rather they are meant for assisting you in remembering that which your heart already knows to be true. Whenever you feel lost, pick up this book, become inspired and rediscover your way home. Love awaits your return." - Yogi Kanna, Author of *Return to Love*

Made in the USA
Lexington, KY
21 May 2014